THE FUTURE
OF
SOUTHEAST ASIAN
COUNTRIES

- Population Change, Climate Change, Management of Japanese Companies and Competitiveness

Edited by

Yasuyuki KOMAKI

YACHIYO SHUPPAN

Copyright © 2018 by Yasuyuki KOMAKI et al.

All rights reserved. No part of this publication may be reproduced or transmitted in any form or by any means, electronic or mechanical, including photocopying, recording, scanning, or any information storage or retrieval system, without written permission from the publisher.

Published by

Yachiyo Shuppan Co., Ltd.

2-2-13 Kandamisakicho Chiyoda-ku Tokyo

Phone 03-3262-0420

Fax 03-3237-0723

www.yachiyo-net.co.jp

ISBN: 978-4-8429-1736-8

First published in JAPAN on December 27, 2018

Preface

In this research, we will discuss important parts such as population in Asia, Climate change, household consumption behavior, advancement of Japanese enterprises, competitiveness in Asian region, input linkage, etc.

We visited 5 countries through this study. Myanmar and Cambodia have gained economic strength. Many large luxury cars were seen in these countries. And as for GDP, all southeast Asia countries exceeds 5000 dollars per capita person around 2015. An economical link between each country rises, and its economic activity, connected continue to be closer relation.

However, most in the Southeast Asian nations has lost the economic growth peaking in around 2008. When we judge by the productive population later, decrease of production population has been begun already in Thailand and China. According to a prediction of UN, the population will decrease from around 2030, and the aging is developed rapidly in the 10 years. The industrial link is high, and when saying, a problem of a country can also be called the problem that I should think in the whole Asian countries.

On the other hand, the climate problems become a big risk on a global scale. Due to the progress of global warming, it is also predicted that coastal areas will submerge. Especially, agricultural products will deteriorate due to abnormal weather. I think that this problem is a very important concern for Japan, too. We hope we will share with you all the various problems in Asia for further advance each research.

Finally, we would like to thank everyone concerned. Especially, this research project is supported by Center for China and Asian Studies grants (currently Center for Global Studies on Culture and Society), when the research representative, Yasuyuki Komaki, belonged to the college of Economics, Nihon University.

Contributors

Yasuyuki KOMAKI
Professor, Faculty of Economics, Osaka University of Economics
Chapter 1

Hiroyuki SHIBUSAWA
Associate Professor, Graduate School of Architecture and Civil Engineering, Toyoyashi University of Technology
Chapter 2, Chapter 4

Sutee ANANTSUKSOMSRI
Lecturer, Department of Urban and Regional Planning, Faculty of Architecture, Chulalongkorn University
Chapter 2

Nij TONTISIRIN
Assistant Professor, Faculty of Architecture and Planning, Thammasat University
Chapter 2

Nattapong PUTTANAPONG
Assistant Professor, Faculty of Economics, Thammasat University
Chapter 2

Yosuke TAKEDA
Professor, Department of Economics, Sophia University
Chapter 3, Chapter 4

Van NGHIEM
Statistician, Department of National Accounts, General Statistics Office, Vietnam   *Chapter 3*

Ichihiro UCHIDA
Professor, Department of Economics, Aichi University
Chapter 3, Chapter 4

Shoichi HISA
Prefessor, Department of Economics, Kanagawa University
Chapter 5, Chapter 6

Yuko HISA
Professor, Department of Economics, Teikyo University
Chapter 5, Chapter 6

Hidenobu OKUDA
Professor, The Graduate School of Economics, Hitotsubashi University   *Chapter 5*

Nariyasu YAMASAWA
Professor, Faculty of Management, Atomi University
Chapter 7

Table of Contents

Preface   i

Chapter 1

The Effect of Demographic Change
on Southeast Asian Developing and Advanced Countries   1

Chapter 2

Evaluating the Spatial Linkages of Thailand's Inter-Provincial
Economies and Industries : An Input-Output Approach   16

Chapter 3

Climate Changes and the Living Standards:
A Regional-Scale Assessment of the Vulnerability in Vietnam   35

Chapter 4

Consumption Smoothing in the Aftermath of the 2014 Coup d'état
in the Thai Urban and Rural Areas : A Preliminary Estimation   52

Chapter 5

Transactions, Network Centrality, and Foreign Direct Investment
As Well As Withdrawal of FDI by Japanese Firms   66

Chapter 6

Dynamics of the Network Structure and Activity of Japanese Firms   78

Chapter 7

Comparison of the Potential Competitiveness of Asian Countries   92

Chapter 1

The Effect of Demographic Change on Southeast Asian Developing and Advanced Countries

Yasuyuki KOMAKI

Abstract

In this paper, we discuss the influence of demographic changes on economic activity in Southeast Asia. In terms of population and economic growth, the economic environment among the Southeast Asia countries differs. In some countries, such as Thailand, the demographic bonus period has ended and there are negative effects from population changes. Meanwhile, in Cambodia and Laos, the bonus period is expected to continue until the 2040s. Thus, there are differences in the region and the degree of the effect of demographic change is likely to expand.

JEL : E0, E3, J10

Keywords : Demographic Change, Population Bonus, Middle-Income Countries, Business Condition

1. Introduction

The United Nations predicts that population in China and Thailand will begin to decline around 2030 and the aging rate will reach the same level as Japan faced in 2014 (United Nations 2017). However, in Southeast Asia countries, except for Thailand and Vietnam, the population will not begin to decline until around 2060. In terms of the ratio of the population aged 65 or older, the ratio reaches 25% at that time. Thus, the influence of demographic change will have an increasing impact in the future.

Many Asian countries have developed successfully, becoming middle-income countries. However, as some countries achieve high economic growth, there are concerns that China and Southeast Asia countries could fall into the middle-income country trap without further transitioning to stable growth. Gill and Kharas (2007) indicate that Thailand, specifically, may fall into this middle-income trap.

One reason to fall into the middle-income country trap, in the case of East and Southeast Asia countries, is the deployment of a growth strategy based on the accumulation of production factors, such as capital stock and labor, which can suppress economic growth gradually due to a decline in the marginal productivity of capital. This seems to be one factor of demographic change that can deteriorate the economic environment in the future.

There has been a good deal of discussion of the "Great Moderation." In the mid-1980s, we saw a reduction in the volatility of business cycle fluctuations. Furthermore, we expected this situation to continue into the future because of institutional and structural changes in developed countries. There are many papers that study the "Great Moderation" that have pointed out that aging and the change in the population composition influence the economic situation directly (Jaimovich and Siu 2009). Subsequently, although we saw a heavy correction based on the so-called Leman shock in 2008, stable and slow business conditions continued in the mid-2010s in the US. Such a period has been called "secular stagnation" as referenced by Summers (2014), as well as others. There are two reasons for secular stagnation. The first concerns the "supply side" of an economy where its capacity to grow becomes impaired, for example, through a decline in the growth of the labor force not offset by an increase in labor productivity. The second reason may arise because productivity-increasing investment has reached its limit and/or measurable technical improvements in products and production processes are also limited.

In this paper, we estimate the effect of demographic change in Southeast Asia countries. In general, demographic change influences both the demand and supply sides of the economy. The following three matters are considered to analyze the characteristics of the effect of demographic change:

(i) We distinguish the stages of economic growth to analyze the effects in Southeast Asia countries. According to previous research, there are countries that may fall into the middle-income trap when GDP exceeds around $10,000 per capita. The level of GDP per capita is very different across the region. In Laos, Cambodia, Vietnam, Myanmar, GDP per capita has stayed around $5,000. On the other hand, in Thailand, the Philippines, Indonesia, and Malaysia, it is over $10,000. Therefore, we divide the estimates into these two groups.

(ii) We analyze the differences between population bonus (the status that the ratio of working-age population increase exceeds the rate of total population expansion due to the fluctuation of population composition, birth rate and death rate) and onus (the status that working-age population dramatically drops and simultaneously population of aged people largely expands) periods in terms of demographic change. According to demographic dynamics, Thailand is in the onus period as is China, but Cambodia and Laos are expected to continue their bonus periods until the mid-2000s.

(iii) We make predictions regarding the future considering only changes in demographics, as we hold the other conditions constant. Due to improvements in the quality of labor input, it is possible that the effects of the population decline and its aging could be offset. Therefore, the results of our estimates are considered to represent the lower expectation of a country's economic growth.

2. Demographics Change and Economic Conditions

2. 1. Population Bonus

Southeast Asian population has continued to slow since around the middle of the 1960s (Figure 1). In contrast, although the production-age population rate began to decline in the 1970s, Asian countries, including Japan, have been achieving sustainable growth, benefiting from "population bonus" (the status where the ratio of the increase in the production-age population exceeds the rate of total population expansion due to the fluctuation in the population composition in terms of the birth and death rates). Figure 2 shows the ratio of the production-age population. This ratio of the production-age population maintains an upward trend, except for in Thailand and China.

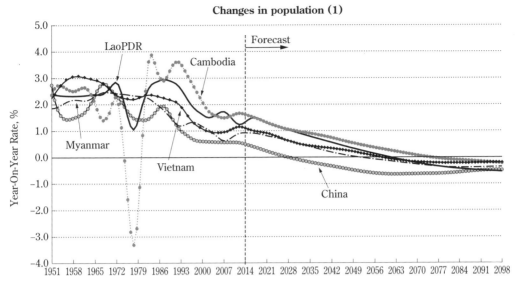

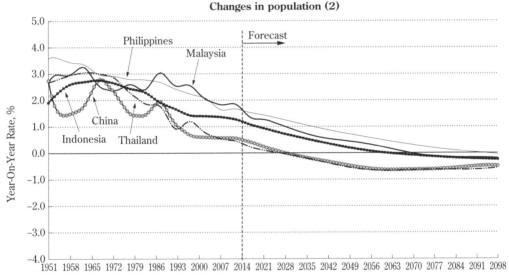

Figure 1 : Change in Population in Southeast Asia Countries

However, regions where the growth in the population is small and there is a labor force shortage receive labor from neighboring areas. For example, Malaysia faced labor shortages in the 1990s and accepted workers from Indonesia and the Philippines. In the first half of the 1990s, many workers from Myanmar flowed into Thailand. With the acceptance of this labor force, the non-skilled, labor-intensive industries can remain competitive.

However, according to the population forecasts in the Asian region, aging is further developed in Thailand and China (Figure 3). In the case of structural changes in the population, Thailand, Vietnam,

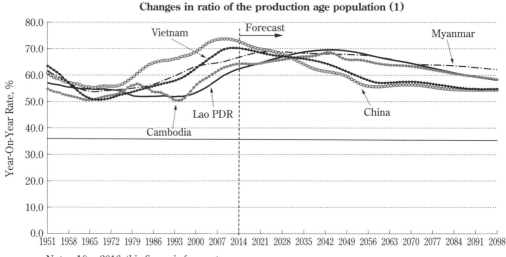

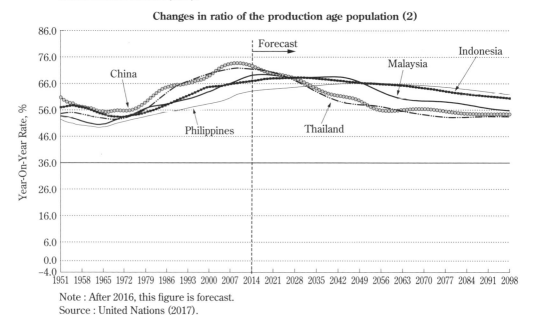

Figure 2 : Change in the Ratio of the Production Age Population

Singapore, and China have almost finished their demographic bonus periods (the period beginning in the year the production-age population ratio begins to decline or increase).

It is estimated that the "population bonus" periods will end in some Asian countries, while in other countries, which have not fully achieved economic success, the "population onus" will hit later (Table 1).

2. 2. Middle-Income Countries

In the Asian region, since the latter half of the 1980s, following Korea and Taiwan, Malaysia, Thailand, and China have developed at a growing pace. Despite the Asian currency crisis in the latter half of the

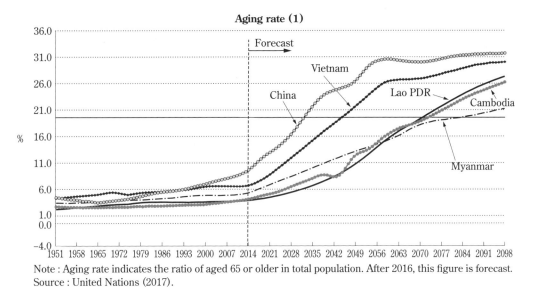

Note : Aging rate indicates the ratio of aged 65 or older in total population. After 2016, this figure is forecast.
Source : United Nations (2017).

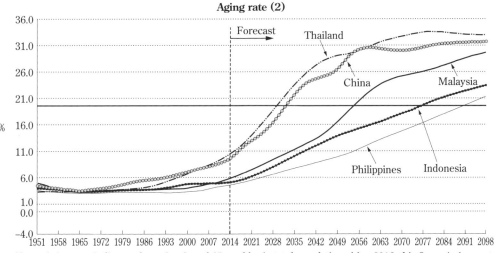

Note : Aging rate indicates the ratio of aged 65 or older in total population. After 2016, this figure is forecast.
Source : United Nations (2017).

Figure 3 : Change in the Aging Rate

Table 1 : The Periods of "Population Bonus"

	Bottom	Peak
Cambodia	1965	2045
Indonesia	1972	2031
Laos	1994	2046
Malaysia	1965	2020
Myanmar	1968	2027
Philippines	1965	2055
Singapore	1964	2011
Thailand	1970	2011
Vietnam	1969	2014
China	1967	2011
Southeastern Asia	1969	2021

Note : this table indicates the next year of the bottom and top peak in the production-age population.
Source : United Nations (2017).

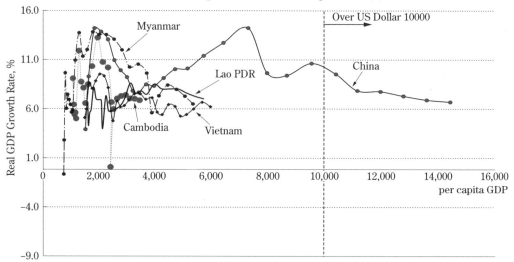

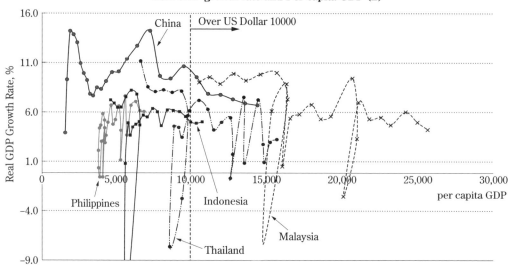

Figure 4 : Change in per Capita GDP

1990s, Indonesia and the Philippines increased their growth potential in the 2000s, while India and Vietnam maintained high growth. In addition, late developing countries, such as Cambodia, Laos, and Bangladesh, have continued their economic growth and, thus, all of Asia has been developing. As a result, all countries are defined as middle-income countries (GDP per capita per country more than $1,045 and less than $12,735 according to the World Bank) in Southeast Asia as of 2017 (Figure 4).

3. The Effect of Demographic Change on the Economy

3. 1. Influence on Economic Activity

The influence of demographic change on economic activity can be divided into supply and demand. In addition, the effect on economic activity may be positive or negative. Furthermore, whether the positive or negative effects will be significant will depend on the disparities in the country's economic structure such as the industries and the locations of the businesses in the region. In general, in areas that include metropolitan sites, there is the possibility that both the supply and the demand sides will see positive effects while the negative effects may be higher in urban areas where aging progresses.

3. 1. 1. Supply Side

As other conditions are held constant, the population decline will reduce the labor force.

In addition, according to the life-cycle hypothesis, savings will decrease due to aging. As a result, the capital formation will be constrained. The effect on capital formation may be similar to the decrease in the labor force. In other words, the economic growth rate will be lower due to the suppression effects of labor and capital. However, due to the progress of technological innovation, such as artificial intelligence, the labor shortage and capital may be offset. In addition, it may be possible to partially promote the employment of women and the elderly to address the decrease in the number of workers. The effects of such alternate solutions for labor and capital shortages will be higher in regions such as metropolitan areas where there are many employment opportunities. As a result, capital investment by private enterprises in metropolitan areas will possibly increase and economic volatility may be higher. On the other hand, in areas where the population declines and aging progresses, it is possible that the GDP growth rate will decline due to the aging of the labor force. Thus, a disparity between regions may expand in the same country.

3. 1. 2. Demand Side

As a declining population leads to a shrinking of the future consumption market, companies are expected to reduce investment and restrain employment. In addition, if a demand shortage is predicted that will continue into the future, wages will not be raised going forward. As a result, demand shortage may lead to. An aging population will lead to an increase in service consumption such as medical treatment. On the other hand, in preparing for retirement based on an increase in longevity risk, the labor force will generate an increase in savings and labor input and the GDP growth rate will increase. From the viewpoint of demand, as stable consumer demand increases, the economic fluctuation will decline as aging progresses. On the other hand, in areas, including cities, the effect of increasing labor input will lead to an increase in the economic growth rate.

3. 2. Demographic Change and Fluctuation Results in Previous Studies

In developed countries, including the US, it has been argued that the economic growth rate and volatility have declined due to a population decrease and the aging of the population. Jaimovich and Siu

(2009) were the first to study the influence of demographic change on business conditions. Subsequently, there have been studies that have clarified the cause of the "Great Moderation" in the US economy.

Jaimovich and Siu (2009) use the working hours of G7 countries as a proxy variable for the business cycle. Volatility[1] is calculated from data on working hours. To estimate the explanatory variable, they model equation (1) using population decomposition.

$$\sigma_{st} = \alpha_s + \beta_t + \gamma share_{st} + \epsilon_{st} \qquad (1)$$

where σ_{st} is volatility in each area s and each period t. $share_{st}$ is the ratio of population decomposition in each area s and each period t. α_{st} is the specific effect on each regional economy. β_t is the fixed effect for time. The estimation period is from 1963 to 2005.

According to estimation results, they point out that the volatility is higher for the young at 4.35 to 2.13%, for the middle-aged, it is low at 0.790 to 0.824%, and it is 1.039 to 2.839% for the pre-retirement age group. Considering the population composition, due to aging, volatility will decline.

Lugauera and Redmonda (2011) use 51 country samples. Volatility is calculated by the same method as in Jaimovich and Siu (2009). They estimate equation (2) by adding the GDP growth rate ($\delta growth_{st}$) as an explanatory variable[2]. The age group (young people) is the percentage of the population aged 15-26 among those aged 15-64.

$$\sigma_{st} = \alpha_s + \beta_t + \delta growth_{st} + \gamma share_{st} + \epsilon_{st} \qquad (2)$$

As in Jaimovich and Siu (2009), this age group (young people) would increase volatility by about 3.92%. In the case that adds economic growth rate as an explanatory variable, the volatility is almost 3.84%.

Lugauera (2012) uses a panel estimation employing state GDP in the US. The estimation period is from 1981 to 2004. The method of measuring volatility is the same as in Jaimovich and Siu (2009). Since the ratio of young people has a high correlation with the past birth rate, they estimate using the birth rate as an instrument variable. The impact of the young people's ratio on the business cycle is 3.13%. The effect value is 5.19% in the case of the instrument variable method.

Maetas et al. (2016) also use panel analysis employing state GDP in the US. They use the average value of 10 years. The estimate method is based on a production function with labor, capital, and technology in addition to the aging rate (the proportion of the population aged 60 or over in the population over 20 years old) as the explanatory variable. According to their results, the economic growth rate will drop by 5.5% due to a 10% aging. In addition, a decline in labor productivity due to aging will reduce the economic growth rate and its effect accounts for about 60% of total growth.

"Secular stagnation" is a major economic issue since Summers (2014) pointed out that economic

---

1 The calculation method of volatility data is as follows. The original data are logarithmically transformed. Subsequently, the original data are smoothed by the Hodrick-Prescott (HP) filter. Next, the gap between the original data and the smoothed data is squared. The central moving average for the gap data on nine years is used as the volatility data. The smoothness parameter of the HP filter is 6.25.

2 Ramey and Ramey (1995) pointed out that there is a negative correlation between economic growth rate and volatility.

fluctuations are stable at a low-level over the long term. Previous studies have been more concerned with the impact on economic structure than demographics. Early studies (Easterly and Levine 2001) have shown that differences between countries are caused by differences in labor productivity and total factor productivity (TFP). Easterly and Levine (2001) analyze the reason for income disparity in each country as macro-based caused by the input of production factors and the difference in TFP.

4. Estimating Methods

4. 1. Data

We analyze nine countries; Cambodia, Indonesia, Laos, Malaysia, Myanmar, Philippines, Thailand, Vietnam, and China. We use GDP from the database of the Asian Development Bank, and Population data from the database of the United Nations. For the per capita GDP (PPP basis, in dollars), we use the "World Development Indicators" from the World Bank. In this study, we adopt panel data analysis using data from 1990 to 2016. We check the estimation method using the Hausman test.

4. 1. 1. Variables for the Aspects of Business Conditions

In this study, we analyze economic fluctuation in terms of three aspects: cycle, trend, and volatility (Figure 5). We use the GDP growth rate (year-over-year growth rate) as the cycle factor to confirm the direction of change. Since the trend factor targets the long-term average fluctuation, excluding seasonality, we use the backward five-year window as the trend component estimated by the HP filter after we logarithmically transform the original data. The smoothness parameter of the HP filter is 100. Volatility data are the squared gap data between the trend and the smoothed data.

4. 1. 2. Demographic Change Variables

It is important how we set the age decomposition as the proxy for demographic change. The production-age population is assumed to be 15 to 64 years old, as commonly referenced in Japan.

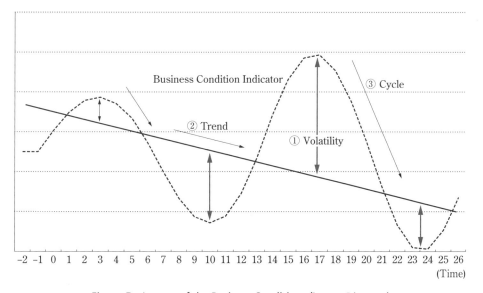

Figure 5 : Aspects of the Business Conditions (Image Diagram)

According to Jaimovich and Siu (2009), we follow the population ratios as ages 20-34 as young people, 35-49 as middle-aged, and 50-64 as elderly people. In addition, assuming a labor force, we use a core data layer of 25-54 years old and the population of 65 years or older (elderly people).

4. 2. Model

According to the MTV (multivariate time series variance component) model (Kariya 1986), we estimate the relation between business cycle indicators and demographic change. We show the equations of business cycle indicators in each area i as follow:

$$x_{it} = \beta_{ij} f_{jt} + u_{it} \tag{3}$$

$$x_{it} = \beta_{i1} f_{1t} + \beta_{i2} f_{2t} + u_{it} \tag{4}$$

where x_{it} is the business cycle indicators and f_{jt} is the fluctuation (economic growth) factor. f_{jt} is divided by trend, cycle, and volatility factors in this study. u_{it} is the disturbance factor.

We regard the factors affecting economic growth in Southeast Asia as a composition of the same factors and several different factors. Several factors are comprised of demographic changes and industrial structure mainly.

We use the age decomposition as a demographic factor, as in Jaimovich and Siu (2009). The youth share denotes the fraction of the total population under the age of 20-34; the middle share denotes those aged 35-49, while the elder share denotes those aged 50-64; the core group denotes those aged 25-54 and the elderly over 65.

In addition to demographic changes, we use industrial structure variables as in Tokui et al. (2013). As it seems that the manufacturing industry is higher in productivity and has a larger effect on business conditions than non-manufacturers, we use the manufacture share in each area.

We estimate equation (5) as the effects of the trend factor, equation (6) as the effects of the cycle, and equation (7) as the effects of volatility. We use the instrument valuables method using birth rate as the instrument value as in Lugauera (2012).

$$Trend_{it} = \alpha_i + \beta_{it} + \gamma Demographics_{it} + Wa_{it} + u_{it} \tag{5}$$

$$Cycle_{it} = \alpha_i + \beta_{it} + \delta Demographics_{it} + Wa_{it} + u_{it} \tag{6}$$

$$Volatility_{it} = \alpha_i + \beta_{it} + \theta Demographics_{it} + Wa_{it} + u_{it} \tag{7}$$

where γ, δ, and θ are parameters. W_t is useful information at time t.

5. Results

The results of the estimates are expressed in terms of the stages of the economic growth in each country and the demographic bonus and onus periods.

5. 1. Effect for Volatility

The effect of economic variability is shown in Table 2. In the cases of less than $10,000 GDP per capita (estimations 1 to 12) and countries in the demographic bonus period (estimations 31 to 36), demographic changes are not affecting the economic fluctuations. However, in areas where GDP per capita exceeds $10,000, it is statistically significant that the increase in the number of young people and the population cause the higher volatility of economic activity (estimations 13-18 and 25-30). This is similar to the results in previous studies such as Lugauera and

Redmonda (2011). However, the estimations including China are not statistically significant (estimations 19-24).

In the population onus regions, we can statistically significantly confirm that the increase in the population and the young population increases the volatility of the economic activity (estimations 37-42). The maturity of the economic environment may also increase the volatility of economic fluctuations.

5. 2. Effect for Trend

The impact on the economic trend is shown in Table 3. In the cases of less than $10,000 GDP per

Table 2 : The Results of the Effect of Volatility

Subject to countries	Per Capita GDP under 10000		Per Capita GDP over 10000			Population Bonus	Population onus
	Cambodia, Laos, Vietnam, Myanmar		Indonesia, Philippines, Malaysia, Thailand	Indonesia, Philippines, Malaysia, Thailand, China	Indonesia, Philippines, Malaysia, Thailand	Cambodia, Indonesia, Laos, Philippines, Malaysia, Myanmar	Thailand, Vietnam
Control Variables		Ratio of Manufacture			Ratio of Manufacture	Ratio of Manufacture	Ratio of Manufacture
Estimation No	1	7	13	19	25	31	37
Population Change	−0.0239 (−0.02387)	−0.0415 (−0.04147)	0.2882 (0.28816)***	0.1755 (0.17551)**	0.0850 (0.08502)	0.0102 (0.01017)	0.2953 (0.29534)***
Estimation No	2	8	14	20	26	32	38
Youth (aged 20-34)	0.0022 (0.00223)	0.0163 (0.01628)	0.0455 (0.04552)***	0.0129 (0.01289)	0.1491 (0.14907)***	0.0147 (0.01465)	0.1090 (0.10902)***
Estimation No	3	9	15	21	27	33	39
Middle (aged 35-49)	0.0016 (0.00157)	0.0117 (0.01172)	−0.0524 (−0.05241)***	−0.0133 (−0.01332)	−0.0373 (−0.03734)***	−0.0030 (−0.00296)	−0.0370 (−0.03697)***
Estimation No	4	10	16	22	28	34	40
Elder (aged 50-64)	−0.0042 (−0.00421)	0.0302 (0.03016)	−0.0500 (−0.04999)***	−0.0092 (−0.00920)	−0.0345 (−0.03454)***	−0.0035 (−0.00350)	−0.0533 (−0.05326)***
Estimation No	5	11	17	23	29	35	41
Core (aged 25-54)	−0.0014 (−0.00136)	0.0071 (0.00711)	−0.0280 (−0.02796)***	−0.0105 (−0.01051)	−0.0180 (−0.01796)	0.0012 (0.00116)	−0.0270 (−0.02696)***
Estimation No	6	12	18	24	30	36	42
Old (over 65)	−0.0110 (−0.01096)	0.0294 (0.02945)	−0.0860 (−0.08600)***	−0.0283 (−0.02831)	−0.0634 (−0.06338)***	0.0162 (0.01618)	−0.0876 (−0.08761)***
Countries	4		4	5	4	6	2
Observation	108		108	135	108	162	54

Note 1 : Explained variable is Trend factor of GRP.
2 : Estimation period : 1990-2016.
3 : Instrument variable is bairth rate.
4 : Figure in parenthesis is standard error.
5 : *, **, *** indicate that the coefficients are statistically different from zero at the 10, 5, and 1 percent level, respectively.

Table 3 : The Results of the Effect of Trend

	Per Capita GDP under 10000		Per Capita GDP over 10000			Population Bonus	Population onus
Subject to countries	Cambodia, Laos,Vietnam, Myanmar		Indonesia, Philippines, Malaysia, Thailand	Indonesia, Philippines, Malaysia, Thailand,China	Indonesia, Philippines, Malaysia, Thailand, China	Cambodia, Indonesia, Laos, Philippines, Malaysia, Myanmar	Thailand. Vietnam, China
Control Variables		Ratio of Manufacture			Ratio of Manufacture	Ratio of Manufacture	Ratio of Manufacture
Estimation No	1	7	13	19	25	31	37
Population Change	−99.1514 (−99.15136)***	14.6127 (14.61271)***	−112.2767 (−112.2760)***	−139.1222 (−139.12220)***	−147.8827 (−147.88270)***	−90.4696 (−90.46957)***	−29.3258 (−29.32575)
Estimation No	2	8	14	20	26	32	38
Youth (aged 20-34)	35.1506 (35.15059)***	26.1203 (26.12029)***	−9.7302 (−9.73025)**	−19.7278 (−19.72783)***	−36.1269 (−36.12690)***	27.8605 (27.86053)***	−41.7401 (−41.74012)***
Estimation No	3	9	15	21	27	33	39
Middle (aged 35-49)	27.6716 (27.67158)***	21.0760 (21.07602)***	15.6249 (15.62486)***	19.4346 (19.43456)***	19.4334 (19.43340)***	28.7492 (28.74917)***	9.5649 (9.56490)***
Estimation No	4	10	16	22	28	34	40
Elder (aged 50-64)	47.7194 (47.71941)***	56.0653 (56.06528)***	16.4928 (16.49275)***	20.5486 (20.54859)***	20.0195 (20.01948)***	33.1670 (33.16700)***	−0.4878 (−0.48781)
Estimation No	5	11	17	23	29	35	41
Core (aged 25-54)	17.7893 (17.78929)***	15.0849 (15.08488)***	11.1285 (11.12845)***	13.3927 (13.39271)***	13.0256 (13.02562)***	17.5087 (17.50868)***	−1.4024 (−1.40244)***
Estimation No	6	12	18	24	30	36	42
Old (over 65)	1.7715 (1.77153)***	2.8031 (2.80310)***	10.0944 (10.09439)***	9.1313 (9.13126)***	15.1420 (15.14195)***	6.1654 (6.16544)***	13.6045 (13.60454)***
Countries	4		4	5		6	3
Observation	108		108	135		162	81

Note 1 : Explained variable is Trend factor of GRP.

    2 : Estimation period :1990-2016.

    3 : Instrument variable is bairth rate.

    4 : Figure in parenthesis is standard error.

    5 : *, **, *** indicate that the coefficients are statistically different from zero at the 10, 5, and 1 percent level, respectively.

capita (estimations 1 to 12), demographic changes have not affected economic fluctuations, especially estimations including the control variable where we see stable results. However, in areas where GDP per capita exceeds $10,000, it is statistically significant that the increase in the population except for the young causes the upward trend of economic activity (estimations 13-30). In both the population bonus and onus periods, we can statistically significantly confirm that the increase in the population leads to an upward trend of economic activity (estimations 31-42).

5. 3. Effect for Cycle

The impact on the economic cycle is shown in Table 4. If per capita GDP is less than $10,000, introducing the control variables obtains statistically meaningful results. In this regard, it can be confirmed that an increase in the manufacturing industry ratio has the effect of enhancing economic growth in the region (estimations 1-12).

On the other hand, if the per capita GDP exceeds $10,000, the estimates without the manufacturing ratio (estimates 13 to 24) are not significant. However, statistically meaningful results are obtained in the estimates using the manufacturing industry ratio and China (estimations 25 to 30). We can confirm that the

Table 4 : The Results of the Effect of Cycle (Growth Rate)

	Per Capita GDP under 10000		Per Capita GDP over 10000			Population Bonus	Population onus
Subject to countries	Cambodia, Laos,Vietnam, Myanmar		Indonesia, Philippines, Malaysia, Thailand	Indonesia, Philippines, Malaysia, Thailand,China	Indonesia, Philippines, Malaysia, Thailand,China	Cambodia, Indonesia, Laos, Philippines, Malaysia, Myanmar	Thailand, Vietnam, China
Control Variables		Ratio of Manufacture			Ratio of Manufacture	Ratio of Manufacture	Ratio of Manufacture
Estimation No	1	7	13	19	25	31	37
Population Change	−0.9003 (−0.90028)*	−1.2815 (−1.28146)*	0.9732 (0.97320)	1.1129 (1.11291)	1.3887 (1.38868)**	−0.7523 (−0.75227)	1.2491 (1.24908)**
Estimation No	2	8	20	26	32	14	38
Youth (aged 20-34)	0.4119 (0.41192)*	0.5937 (0.59366)	1.0825 (1.08247)**	0.6924 (0.69236)**	0.7386 (0.73858)**	0.7820 (0.78202)***	0.7198 (0.71982)**
Estimation No	3	9	15	21	27	33	39
Middle (aged 35-49)	0.1081 (0.10814)	0.4910 (0.49101)**	−0.4351 (−0.43507)**	−0.2356 (−0.23556)	−0.3043 (−0.30428)**	0.4681 (0.46805)***	−0.3909 (−0.39088)**
Estimation No	4	10	16	22	28	34	40
Elder (aged 50-64)	0.4472 (0.44716)*	0.9333 (0.93335)**	−0.2406 (−0.24058)	−0.3123 (−0.31231)**	−0.3158 (−0.31580)**	0.6076 (0.60756)***	−0.6089 (−0.60894)***
Estimation No	5	11	17	23	29	35	41
Core (aged 25-54)	0.1361 (0.13615)*	0.2404 (0.24040)**	−0.2862 (−0.28620)**	−0.2020 (−0.20200)**	−0.1590 (−0.15901)**	0.2333 (0.23333)***	−0.3354 (−0.33535)***
Estimation No	6	12	18	24	30	36	42
Old (over 65)	0.4353 (0.43527)	0.5259 (0.52591)	−0.8552 (−0.85519)**	−0.4248 (−0.42475)	−0.5835 (−0.58346)*	1.2491 (1.24908)**	−0.8739 (−0.87390)***
Countries	4		4	5		6	3
Observation	108		108	135		162	81

Note 1 : Explained variable is Trend factor of GRP.
    2 : Estimation period :1990-2016.
    3 : Instrument variable is bairth rate.
    4 : Figure in parenthesis is standard error.
    5 : *, **, *** indicate that the coefficients are statistically different from zero at the 10, 5, and 1 percent level, respectively.

increase in the population and in the younger generation significantly increase the economic growth rate.

In the demographic bonus period, increasing young people and older people can be seen to increase economic growth (estimations 31-36). This result is similar to Jaimovich and Siu (2009). However, in the demographic onus period, only young population growth increases economic growth (estimations 37-42).

5. 4. Summary

In general, in population onus periods where the per capita GDP exceeds $10,000, increasing the youth population leads to a greater change and volatility in the country's economic condition. This is the same stage that has been the target of previous research. On the other hand, in population bonus, periods, almost every population decomposition leads to higher volatility in the country's economic condition. However, where there is per capita GDP less than $10,000, the estimates are not significant.

6. Conclusion

In this paper, we address the influence of demographic changes on economic activity. In terms of population and economic growth, the economic environment among Southeast Asian countries differs. In some countries, such as Thailand, the demographic bonus period has ended and negative effects from population changes may have an impact. Meanwhile, in Cambodia and Laos, the bonus period is expected to continue until the 2040s. Thus, there are differences in the region and the degree of the effect of demographic change is likely to expand in the future.

In the population onus regions with per capita GDP exceeding $10,000, an increase in the population and the young leads to a boost in economic growth. On the other hand, for Cambodia, Laos, and Myanmar, the population bonus periods will continue into the future. Therefore, it seems the economic activity in these countries will improve as their economic growth rates increase.

However, in Myanmar and Malaysia, the population bonus periods are expected to end in the 2020s. This is nearly 20 years earlier than the other two countries. In this respect, economic structural reform is required immediately in Myanmar and Malaysia.

In addition, in the case of the potential middle-income trap, a declining population and an aging labor force will have a significant effect. According to demographic change alone, Thailand and Vietnam, which are in population onus periods, seem to face a substantial risk of falling into middle-income country traps in the future.

References

Easterly, W., and R. Levine (2001), "What Have We Learned from a Decade of Empirical Research on Growth? It's Not Factor Accumulation: Stylized Facts and Growth Models," *World Bank Economic Review*, 15(2), pp.177-219.

Gill, I., and H. Kharas (2007), "An East Asian Renaissance," *The International Bank for Reconstruction and Development,* Washington, DC: The World Bank.

Jaimovich, N., and H. E. Siu (2009), "The Young, the Old, and the Restless: Demographics and Business Cycle Volatility," *American Economic Review*, 99(3), pp.804-826.

Kariya, T. (1986), "Concept and Actuality of Econometric Analysis," *Toyo Keizai* (in Japanese).

Komaki, Y. (2015), "Economic Data and Policy Decision," *Nihon Keizai Shimbun* (in Japanese).

Lugauera, S. (2012), "Estimating the Effect of the Age Distribution on Cyclical Output Volatility Across the United States," *The Review of Economics and Statistics*, 94(4), pp.896-902.

Lugauera, S., and M. Redmonda (2011), "The Age Distribution and Business Cycle Volatility: International Evidence," *WP*, pp.1-8.

Maestas, N., K. J. Mullen, and D. Powell (2016), "The Effect of Population Aging on Economic Growth, The Labor Force and Productivity," *NBER Working Papers*, 22452, p.54.

Summers, L. (2014), "U.S. Economic Prospects: Secular Stagnation, Hysteresis, and the Zero Lower Bound," *Business Economics*, 49(2), pp.65-73.

Tokui, J., T. Makino, K. Fukao, T. Miyagawa, N. Arai, S. Arai, T. Inui, K. Kawasaki, N. Kodama, and N. Noguchi

(2013), "Compilation of the Regional-Level Japan Industrial Productivity Database (R-JIP)," RIETI Discussion Paper Series, 13-J-037 (full paper in Japanese, abstract in English).

United Nations (2017), *World Population Prospects: The 2017 Revision*, DVD Edition, Department of Economic and Social Affairs, Population Division.

Chapter 2

Evaluating the Spatial Linkages of Thailand's Inter-Provincial Economies and Industries: An Input-Output Approach

Hiroyuki SHIBUSAWA, Sutee ANANTSUKSOMSRI,
Nij TONTISIRIN, and Nattapong PUTTANAPONG

Abstract

This paper evaluates the spatial linkages of Thailand's regional economy at the provincial level. A multi-regional input-output (MRIO) table and an inter-regional input-output (IRIO) table are estimated using a non-survey approach. To identify the spatial interdependence among industries at the provincial level, regional multiplier, spillover, and feedback effects are measured using the IRIO model. We examine the relative importance of each province via the hypothetical extraction process of the MRIO model. The influence of Thailand's regional economies is made clear by comparative analysis of the provincial results.

JEL : R12, R15

Keywords : Spatial Linkages, Province Model, Thailand, Regional Economy, Input-Output Table, Multiplier Analysis, Hypothetical Extraction Method

1. Introduction

Thailand is a growing economy in Asia. The capital, Bangkok has witnessed a dramatic transformation in recent years, becoming a global metropolis. The high and ever-increasing population density of this metropolis has long been a concern because of the large income discrepancy between urban and rural residents. The Department of Public Works and Town & Country Planning (DPT) established a national-regional plan to implement development policies, strategies, and frameworks for spatial development and planning (MLIT 2017). The project includes a policy plan spanning 50 years (2006-2056).

Input-output analysis is widely applied for economic development at many geographic levels. In this paper, we develop methodology for evaluating the impact of spatial linkages on regional economies at a provincial level. A multi-regional input-output table (MRIO) and an inter-regional input-output (IRIO) table are estimated using a non-survey approach. To identify the interdependence among industries at the provincial level, regional multiplier, spillover, and feedback effects are measured using the MRIO model. We examine the relative importance of each province via a hypothetical extraction process using the MRIO model. The study critically analyzes the characteristics of inter-provincial economies and industries.

Input-output models for regions can be divided into two types. The IRIO was first described by Isard (1951) and it is often called the "Isard Model". With IRIO models we assume that commodity imports are not domestically produced, instead they are a competitive import type. The MRIO was developed by Chenery (1953) and Moses (1955), and it is often called the "Chenery-Moses model". Under this

Chapter 2 Evaluating the Spatial Linkages of Thailand's Inter-Provincial Economies and Industries: An Input-Output Approach   17

framework, a competitive import is not assumed and commodity imports are treated as if they are domestically produced. The former can capture detailed information about inter-regional trade and the latter provides a powerful tool for analyzing the impacts of changes in inter-regional trade coefficients on regional economies.

The government of Thailand has published a national input-output table, for which national policies and projects have been evaluated. Akiyama (1996) estimated an IRIO table using the table from 1989. This national table was divided into seven regions and 20 production sectors. Akiyama analyzed the decentralization policy of Thailand using the MRIO model. Sim et al. (2007) constructed a modified IRIO table to link the Mukdahan provincial economy with the economy of neighboring Savannakhet province in the Lao People's Democratic Republic. This was a unique study that measured economic dependence between regions located in different Asian countries. Bunditsakulchai (2016) discussed the significance of constructing the IRIO table for analyzing the linkage between regional economies of Thailand. He pointed out that the current tools available for analysis were insufficient for identifying spatial effects at the provincial level. Thus, there was a need for new studies to develop MRIO and IRIO tables and models for Thailand.

This study employs a gravity model and an RAS method to estimate a MRIO table for Thailand's provinces. It incorporates the MRIO model, and a hypothetical extraction method is applied. An IRIO table is then also derived from the MRIO table. A method for comparing the characteristics of provincial industrial structures from the standpoint of multiplier analysis is also developed (Shibusawa et al. 2018).

Chapter 2 describes an estimation method for constructing an IRIO table and a MRIO table for the provincial level in Thailand. In Chapter 3, the multiplier effects of intra-regional, spillover, and feedback are estimated under the IRIO model specification. In Chapter 4, using the MRIO model, the hypothetical extraction method is employed to assess the relative importance of each province in respect to the regional economy. Finally, this study is concluded in Chapter 5.

2. Estimation of IRIO and MRIO Tables for Thailand

There are two approaches used in IRIO and MRIO modeling and thus, two kinds of input-output tables. Tables 1 and 2 show skeletons of the IRIO table and the MRIO table respectively. In the IRIO table, we require a complete set of both intra- and inter-regional trade data. In practice, at the provincial level it is impossible to get very detailed information. Alternative approaches use the MRIO table, which requires inter-regional flows among provinces. However, this data is unavailable in Thailand. In this paper, following the studies of Leontief and Strout (1963), the MRIO and IRIO tables are estimated via non-survey means.

Our study uses the 2005 input-output table for Thailand (purchaser' price table). As shown in Figure 1, Thailand has 76 provinces and the economy is classified by 24 industrial sectors. An overview of the estimation method is provided as follows (Leontief and Strout 1963; Miller and Blair 2009; Yamada and Owaki 2012):

Procedure 1 : Use the 2005 input-output table for Thailand

Table 1 : IRIO Table

		Intermediate demand				Final demand		Imports	Export	Total demand
		Region r		Region s		Regional demand				
		sec1	sec2	sec1	sec2	r	s			
Region r	1	Z_{11}^{rr}	Z_{12}^{rr}	Z_{11}^{rs}	Z_{12}^{rs}	F_1^{rr}	F_1^{rs}	EX_1^r	$-IM_1^r$	X_1^r
	2	Z_{21}^{rr}	Z_{22}^{rr}	Z_{21}^{rs}	Z_{22}^{rs}	F_2^{rr}	F_2^{rs}	EX_2^r	$-IM_2^r$	X_2^r
Region s	1	Z_{11}^{sr}	Z_{12}^{sr}	Z_{11}^{ss}	Z_{12}^{ss}	F_1^{sr}	F_1^{ss}	EX_1^s	$-IM_1^s$	X_1^s
	2	Z_{21}^{sr}	Z_{22}^{sr}	Z_{21}^{ss}	Z_{22}^{ss}	F_2^{sr}	F_2^{ss}	EX_2^s	$-IM_2^s$	X_2^s
Value-added		V_1^r	V_2^r	V_1^s	V_2^s					
Output		X_1^r	X_2^r	X_1^s	X_2^s					

Table 2 : MRIO Table

Region r	Intermediate demand		Final demand	Regional exports		Regional imports		Exports	Imports	Total demand
	sec1	sec2		r	s	r	s			
sec1	Z_{11}^r	Z_{12}^r	F_1^r		T_1^{rs}		$-T_1^{sr}$	EX_1^r	$-IM_1^r$	X_1^r
sec2	Z_{21}^r	Z_{22}^r	F_2^r		T_2^{rs}		$-T_2^{sr}$	EX_2^r	$-IM_2^r$	X_2^r
Value-added	V_1^r	V_2^r								
Output	X_1^r	X_2^r								

Region s	Intermediate demand		Final demand	Regional exports		Regional imports		Exports	Imports	Total demand
	sec1	sec2		r	s	r	s			
sec1	Z_{11}^s	Z_{12}^s	F_1^s	T_1^{sr}		$-T_1^{rs}$		EX_1^s	$-IM_1^s$	X_1^s
sec2	Z_{21}^s	Z_{22}^s	F_2^s	T_2^{sr}		$-T_2^{rs}$		EX_2^s	$-IM_2^s$	X_2^s
Value-added	V_1^s	V_2^s								
Output	X_1^s	X_2^s								

Procedure 2 : Determine the share of each socioeconomic variable for Thailand. Use these share parameters to create an auxiliary MRIO table for each province

Procedure 3 : Use a gravity model and the RAS method to derive the amount of trade between provinces and estimate a MRIO table for each. Subsequently, find the inter-provincial trade coefficient

Procedure 4 : Perform a simple estimation for an IRIO table for provinces, using MRIO tables

There is no data available on trade among the provinces of Thailand. Thus, trade is assumed to depend on the distance between the provinces and the scale of trade (total imports and exports) at the origin and destination. Therefore, as a reference, this paper uses a gravity model, estimated using data from nine regional input-output tables in Japan. Gravity models are derived from Newton's law of universal gravitation. The sum of the rows and columns in the transaction price matrix do not correspond to the standard export and import totals. Therefore, the RAS method was used to adjust them through repetitive calculations until they corresponded. Provinces from Thailand were separated using information pertaining to population, the government budget, and the construction sector of gross provincial products, etc.

Chapter 2 Evaluating the Spatial Linkages of Thailand's Inter-Provincial Economies and Industries: An Input-Output Approach

Figure 1 : Provinces of Thailand (ref. Wikipedia)

3. Inter-Regional Input-Output Analysis

3. 1. Multiplier Effects Model

The backward linkage effect of the IRIO model is given by

$$X=[I-(A-\widehat{M}A^*)]^{-1}(Fi-\widehat{M}F^*i+EX).\qquad(1)$$

This equation has the following elements: X is the production amount column vector; A is the inter-regional input coefficient matrix; $\widehat{M}$ is the import ratio matrix (the import ratio is a diagonal element); F is the final demand matrix; EX is the export amount row vector; I is the identity matrix; and i is the row vector for column sums. An asterisk indicates a diagonal block matrix of regional information given as a diagonal block variable.

Multiplier effects include intra-regional effects that concern only industrial trade within a region, spillover effects that impact several other regions, and feedback effects that return after having been disseminated from that region into a number of other regions. Multiplier analysis typically uses strict factoring methods for two regions, but this paper applies multiplier analysis using a simplified method, because of the greater number of regions.

Multiplier analysis, using this simplified method for IRIO, is applied using the following equation:

$$X=B\overline{F}=\overline{M}_1\overline{F}+\overline{M}_2\overline{F}+\overline{M}_3\overline{F}.\qquad(2)$$

Here, $B=[I-(A-\overline{M}A^*)]^{-1}$ is a Leontief inverse matrix, which denotes an inter-industry multiplier effect in each region. $\overline{F}=(Fi-\widehat{M}F^*i+EX)$ is the total demand inside and outside a region. In the case of n regions, the matrices, X and $\overline{F}$, are given as

$$X=\begin{bmatrix} X^1 \\ \cdots \\ X^n \end{bmatrix},\text{ and }\overline{F}=\begin{bmatrix} \overline{F}^1 \\ \cdots \\ \overline{F}^n \end{bmatrix}.$$

The Leontief inverse matrix, B, is sub-divided into a regional multiplier, $\overline{M}_1$, a spillover effect multiplier, $\overline{M}_2$, and a feedback effect multiplier, $\overline{M}_3$. Resulting in

$$B=\begin{bmatrix} \widetilde{B}^{11} & \cdots & \widetilde{B}^{1n} \\ \vdots & \ddots & \vdots \\ \widetilde{B}^{n1} & \cdots & \widetilde{B}^{nn} \end{bmatrix},$$

$$\overline{M}_1=\begin{bmatrix} B^{11} & \cdots & 0 \\ \vdots & \ddots & \vdots \\ 0 & \cdots & B^{nn} \end{bmatrix},$$

$$\bar{M}_2 = \begin{bmatrix} 0 & \cdots & \widetilde{B}^{1n} \\ \vdots & \ddots & \vdots \\ \widetilde{B}^{n1} & \cdots & 0 \end{bmatrix},$$

$$\bar{M}_3 = \begin{bmatrix} \widetilde{B}^{11} - B^{11} & \cdots & 0 \\ \vdots & \ddots & \vdots \\ 0 & \cdots & \widetilde{B}^{nn} - B^{nn} \end{bmatrix}.$$

$\widetilde{B}^{rs} (r,s=1,\cdots,n)$ is a regional block matrix of a Leontief inverse matrix in the inter-regional table, denoting a multiplier effect for a region ($r=s$) and inter-region ($r \neq s$). The Leontief inverse matrix for the regional table is calculated as

$$B^{rr} = (I - (A^{rr} - \widehat{M}^{rr} A^{*rr}))^{-1}), \tag{3}$$

and it denotes a multiplier effect only within the region.

3. 2. Measuring Multiplier Effects

We determined the regional effect, $\bar{M}_1 \bar{F}$, the spillover effect, $\bar{M}_2 \bar{F}$, and the feedback effect, $\bar{M}_3 \bar{F}$, induced by demand $\bar{F}$ and their respective shares of the total multiplier effect. Figure 2 illustrates the totals for each Thai province, whereas Figure 3 illustrates the totals for each sector.

The top five provinces inducing production (Figure 2) are as follows: Bangkok; Samut Prakarn; Rayong; Phra Nakhon Si Ayudhya; Chonburi; and Samut Sakhon. There is certainly a significant concentration of production inducement in Bangkok. Considering the proportional sizes of the regional, spillover, and feedback effects within Thailand, the regional effect is substantial at 50-70%. The spillover effect is 20-50% and the feedback effect is minor (i.e. less than a few percent). The spillover effect is small because provinces with a large regional effect have a small spillover effect (the sum of the regional, spillover and feedback effects is 100%). The aggregates for all provinces are 59.1% for regional effects, 39.2% for spillover effects and 1.7% for feedback effects.

With regard to the spillover effects, the following provinces exhibited high proportions: Rayong at 53.6%; Kanchanabur at 50.9%; Ang Thong at 50.5%; Suphanburi at 50.1%; and Phangnga at 50.0%. The spillover effects were relatively small in the following provinces: Phuket (16.9%); Chiang Mai (22.7%); Ubon Ratchathani (23%), Udon Thani (24.0%); and Lamphun (25.1%). A small spillover effect implies that the regional effect will be large, and one can observe that the local economies (e.g., Phuket, Chiang Mai and Ubon Ratchathani) have a circular structure. Similarly, provinces with large spillover effects exhibit a relatively strong interdependence with other provinces.

Relatively large feedback effects were observed in Bangkok (3.4%), Samut Prakarn (2.6%), Phra Nakhon Si Ayudhya (2.0%), Chonburi (1.9%), and Rayong (1.8%). Provinces where the total multiplier effect was strong tended to exhibit large feedback effects. This is perhaps because these are regions where many companies producing final goods have larger feedback effects.

As indicated in Figure 3, the top five sectors with respect to the amount of production inducement,

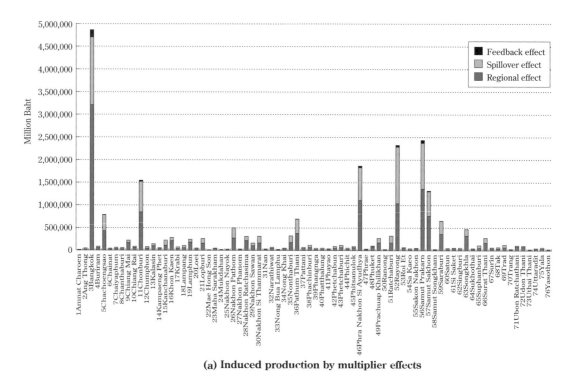

(a) Induced production by multiplier effects

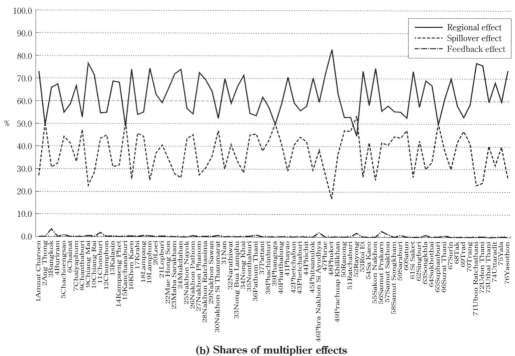

(b) Shares of multiplier effects

Figure 2 : Multiplier effects by province in Thailand

Chapter 2 Evaluating the Spatial Linkages of Thailand's Inter-Provincial Economies and Industries: An Input-Output Approach

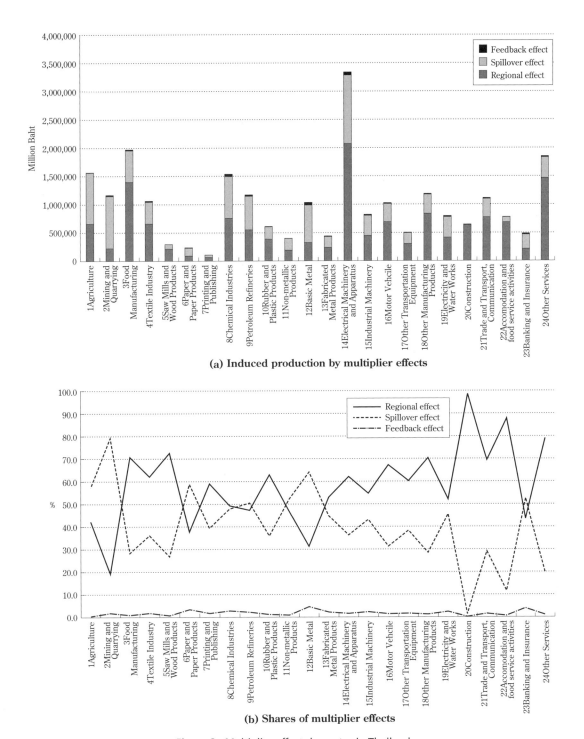

Figure 3 : Multiplier effects by sector in Thailand

for all effects, in Thailand are electrical machinery and apparatus, food manufacturing, other services, agriculture, and chemical industries.

Regarding the share of effects in each sector, regional effects tend to be larger than spillover effects. However, these differ by sector. Spillover effects were larger in mining and quarrying at 79.1%, basic metal at 64.1%, paper and paper products at 58.8%, and agriculture at 57.3%. The share of spillover effects was small in construction at 1.3%, accommodation and food service activities at 11.6%, other services at 19.9%, saw mills and wood products at 26.8%, and food manufacturing at 28.3%. Service industries with a lot of reliance on other regions had small spillover effects.

The feedback effect was large for basic metal at 4.6%, banking and insurance at 3.9%, paper and paper products at 3.4%, chemical industries at 2.8%, and electricity and water works at 2.4%. These industries are more concentrated in urban areas rather than rural areas.

4. Multi-Regional Input-Output Analysis

The hypothetical extraction method is employed to assess the economic importance of provinces. When considering trade relations between industries, one looks at the position of each province. This allows us to assess each province by economic importance, as well as the economic loss incurred by the surrounding provinces in the event that production activities, exports and imports are lost.

4. 1. Hypothetical Extraction Method

In the initial phases of the hypothetical extraction method, the approach is to quantify how much the total output of an n-sector economy would change (decrease), provided a sector (e.g., the jth) was removed from the economy. This procedure was incorporated into a national input-output model by deleting the jth row and the jth column from the input coefficient matrix (Miller and Lahr 2001; Miller and Blair 2009). This paper uses a MRIO model to measure changes in output when a specific region (i.e., province) is extracted or eliminated from the economy.

The backward linkage effect of the MRIO model is provided by the following equation:

$$X = [I - \{TA - \widehat{M}(TA)^*\}]^{-1}(\{TF - \widehat{M}(TF)^*\} + EX). \qquad (4)$$

Here, X is the production value column vector; A is the input coefficient matrix; I is the unit matrix; T is the inter-regional trade coefficient matrix; $\widehat{M}$ is the import ratio matrix; F is the intra-regional final demand column vector; and EX is the export column vector.

In a MRIO, inter-regional trade relations are expressed by inter-regional trade coefficients. A particular region (e.g., the jth), can be excluded or eliminated by setting its inter-regional trade coefficient to zero. This procedure was incorporated into an IRIO model by deleting the jth row and the jth column from the inter-regional trade coefficient matrix. For example, considering three regions, the inter-regional trade coefficient matrix is indicated by the following equation.

Chapter 2 Evaluating the Spatial Linkages of Thailand's Inter-Provincial Economies and Industries: An Input-Output Approach 25

$$T = \begin{pmatrix} t_{11} & t_{12} & t_{13} \\ t_{21} & t_{22} & t_{23} \\ t_{31} & t_{32} & t_{33} \end{pmatrix}.$$

If region 1 is excluded, the trade coefficient matrix is given as

$$T(1) = \begin{pmatrix} 0 & 0 & 0 \\ 0 & t_{22} & t_{23} \\ 0 & t_{32} & t_{33} \end{pmatrix}.$$

Similarly, if region 2 is excluded, the matrix is given as

$$T(2) = \begin{pmatrix} t_{11} & 0 & t_{13} \\ 0 & 0 & 0 \\ t_{31} & 0 & t_{33} \end{pmatrix}.$$

If both regions 1 and 2 are excluded,

$$T(1\&2) = \begin{pmatrix} 0 & 0 & 0 \\ 0 & 0 & 0 \\ 0 & 0 & t_{33} \end{pmatrix}.$$

Elimination of a region is defined as the exclusion of all intra- and inter-regional trading (i.e., imports and exports).

The backward linkage effect of an excluded region is provided by the following equation.

$$\boldsymbol{X}(e) = [\boldsymbol{I} - \{\boldsymbol{T}(e)\boldsymbol{A} - \widehat{\boldsymbol{M}}(\boldsymbol{T}(e)\boldsymbol{A})^*\}]^{-1}(\{\boldsymbol{T}(e)\boldsymbol{F}(e) - \widehat{\boldsymbol{M}}(\boldsymbol{T}(e)\boldsymbol{F}(e))^*\} + \boldsymbol{EX}(e)). \tag{5}$$

Here, $\boldsymbol{F}(e)$ and $\boldsymbol{EX}(e)$, the final demand imports and exports in region e, are set to zero. Based on the definition of $\boldsymbol{T}(e)$, effects will differ when, for example, regions 1 and 2 are extracted simultaneously versus when they are extracted one at a time (i.e., $\boldsymbol{X}(1) + \boldsymbol{X}(2) \neq \boldsymbol{X}(1 \& 2)$).

The percentage decrease in the production of a region's sectors, when a region has been excluded is given by the following equation:

$$D_i^r(e) = \frac{X_i^r - X_i^r(e)}{X_i^r} \times 100. \tag{6}$$

When viewed by regional sector, the importance of trade relations for all industries is shown for that region. Similarly, when a region is excluded, the percentage decrease in production for each and all regions and sectors are defined as follows:

Region r $\quad D^r(e) = \dfrac{\sum_i X_i^r - \sum_i X_i^r(e)}{\sum_i X_i^r} \times 100$

$$\text{Sector } i \quad D_i(e) = \frac{\sum_r X_i^r - \sum_r X_i^r(e)}{\sum_r X_i^r} \times 100$$

$$\text{All regions, All sectors} \quad D(e) = \frac{\sum_i \sum_r X_i^r - \sum_i \sum_r X_i^r(e)}{\sum_i \sum_r X_i^r} \times 100.$$

4. 2. Measuring the Economic Effects of Eliminating Provinces from the National Economy

Figure 4 shows the percentage decrease in total production when various provinces are excluded (i.e., eliminated) from Thailand. Excluding Bangkok has the greatest impact overall, at 36.0%, followed by Samut Prakarn at 18.0%, Rayong at 13.8%, Phra Nakhon Si Ayudhya at 12.9%, and Chonburi at 12.6%.

Table 3 shows the percentage decrease in production by provinces when those in Thailand are eliminated/excluded from analysis. The vertical axis indicates the eliminated provinces, whereas the horizontal axis shows which provinces are more heavily impacted on by their elimination. The values in the figure are percentages. For example, when Bangkok is excluded, its production drops by 100%. The items on the diagonal show that production dropped 100% in the eliminated provinces. Moreover, the row for Bangkok shows a 6% drop in production for Amnat Charoen, a 17% drop for Ang Thong, and a 9% drop for Buriram when Bangkok is eliminated. The biggest drops are a 41% decline for Samut Prakarn, a 35% decline for Nonthaburi, and a 33% decline for Pathum Thani. This shows that these provinces are heavily dependent on Bangkok.

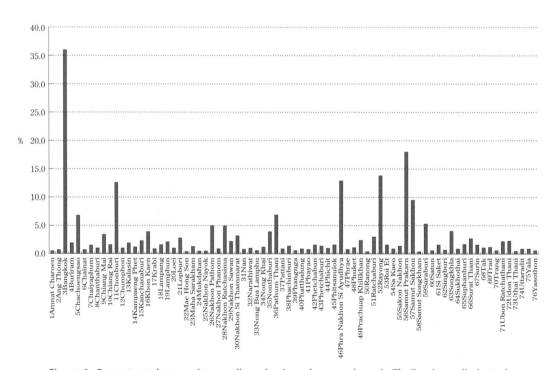

Figure 4 : Percentage decrease in overall production when provinces in Thailand are eliminated

Chapter 2   Evaluating the Spatial Linkages of Thailand's Inter-Provincial Economies and Industries: An Input-Output Approach   27

Table 3 is shaded to show increasingly larger percentage declines in production, progressing from white to black. The items on the diagonal are dark black, representing a 100% decrease in production for that region. Considering the rows, the various provinces with a reddish tint can be regarded as those "of relatively high importance" to Thailand (e.g., Bangkok). Similarly, the rows that are mostly gray indicate provinces that are "of moderate importance." Those with white cells denote provinces "of relatively low importance".

Table 4 indicates the percentage decrease in production by sector when provinces in Thailand are eliminated. The vertical axis shows the eliminated provinces, while the horizontal axis shows how production sectors are affected by the removal of those provinces from the analysis. The unit used in the figure is the percentage decrease in production. For example, considering the rows, the sectors most impacted by eliminating Bangkok are banking and insurance at 64%; followed by accommodation and food service activities at 64%, and trade, transport, and communication at 56%.

The columns in the figure show the degree of impact on a sector when provincial production is eliminated. For example, production in motor vehicles reduces by 40% with the elimination of Samut Prakarn, followed by Bangkok at 37%, Samut Sakhon at 23%, Pathum Thani at 14%, and Phra Nakhon Si Ayudhya at 13%. Many automotive companies are located in these provinces. Eliminating Bangkok leads to a 64% drop in production in banking and insurance, followed by a 12% drop in Samut Prakarn, and a 10% drop in Chonburi. Additionally, production in mining and quarrying reduces by 71% with the elimination of Rayong.

5. Conclusion

Economic development varies widely across space. In Thailand, economic concentration varies across space. Bangkok is a particularly highly concentrated economic area. There has been little work incorporating other spaces, especially regional spatial linkages, into the Thai economy. This paper compiled IRIO and MRIO tables at the provincial level for Thailand. An attempt was made to compare the characteristics of spatial interdependence and industrial structures in provinces by applying a multiplier analysis and a hypothetical extraction method to IRIO and MRIO models. This paper offers a visual representation of economic interdependency characteristics among provinces. Expanding the methodologies may enable a more comprehensive assessment of collaborative efforts between specific or multiple regions and a decentralization development policy in Thailand (Unger and Mahakanjana 2016).

Additionally, this methodology can be applied to measuring the impact of economic losses in the event of natural disasters. In Thailand, floods are regularly occurring natural disasters. Severe flooding impacted the regional economy of Thailand during the 2011 monsoon season. These floods spread through 56 provinces, including Bangkok along the Mekong and Chao Phraya river basins. The World Bank estimated US$ 64.5 billion in economic damage as a result of the floods. Disruption of manufacturing supply chains are affected, not only the regional production activities but also at the global economy level. This paper assumed a complete stoppage of economic activities in a specific province and by

Table 3 : Percentage Decrease in Production by Province When Provinces in Thailand are Eliminated

Columns (left → right) = Extracted Province 1–40; Rows = Province affected.
(1 Annat Charoen, 2 Ang Thong, 3 Bangkok, 4 Buriram, 5 Chachoengsao, 6 Chainat, 7 Chaiyaphum, 8 Chanthaburi, 9 Chiang Mai, 10 Chiang Rai, 11 Chonburi, 12 Chumphon, 13 Kalasin, 14 Kampaeng Phet, 15 Kanchanaburi, 16 Khon Kaen, 17 Krabi, 18 Lampang, 19 Lamphun, 20 Loei, 21 Lopburi, 22 Mae Hong Son, 23 Maha Sarakham, 24 Mukdahan, 25 Nakhon Nayok, 26 Nakhon Pathom, 27 Nakhon Phanom, 28 Nakhon Ratchasima, 29 Nakhon Sawan, 30 Nakhon Si Thammarat, 31 Nan, 32 Narathiwat, 33 Nong Bua Lamphu, 34 Nong Khai, 35 Nonthaburi, 36 Pathum Thani, 37 Pattani, 38 Phachinburi, 39 Phangnga, 40 Phatthalung)

Province	1	2	3	4	5	6	7	8	9	10	11	12	13	14	15	16	17	18	19	20	21	22	23	24	25	26	27	28	29	30	31	32	33	34	35	36	37	38	39	40
1 Annat Charoen	100	0	0	2	3	1	1	0	2	1	2	0	5	1	5	1	0	1	1	1	1	0	1	5	0	0	4	4	1	1	1	0	1	2	1	1	0	1	0	0
2 Ang Thong	0	100	1	0	0	1	1	1	0	0	0	1	1	1	2	0	0	1	1	0	4	0	1	0	4	1	1	4	1	3	2	0	0	1	3	0	0	1	0	0
3 Bangkok	0	17	100	9	18	14	8	14	4	7	17	14	6	8	18	6	12	8	5	10	12	7	6	5	20	24	7	9	11	12	7	12	7	6	35	33	9	16	14	9
4 Buriram	3	2	2	100	2	2	3	3	1	1	2	1	2	2	2	2	2	1	1	2	2	1	4	2	3	3	2	9	2	1	2	2	2	2	1	1	2	4	1	1
5 Chachoengsao	1	3	3	2	100	2	2	6	1	1	9	3	1	2	1	1	2	1	1	2	3	1	1	1	6	1	1	3	2	1	2	2	1	1	3	3	2	11	3	2
6 Chainat	1	2	1	2	0	100	2	1	0	0	0	1	1	2	1	0	1	0	1	1	2	1	3	0	1	1	0	4	3	1	0	1	1	2	1	1	1	1	0	0
7 Chaiyaphum	1	1	2	3	2	1	100	2	0	0	1	1	2	0	0	5	1	1	1	3	2	1	0	1	2	1	0	4	1	1	0	1	3	0	1	1	0	1	1	1
8 Chanthaburi	0	1	2	1	1	1	0	100	0	0	2	1	0	0	0	0	1	1	1	0	0	0	0	1	7	1	0	1	0	1	0	0	0	0	2	1	2	2	1	0
9 Chiang Mai	2	2	2	2	2	3	3	2	100	15	2	2	2	6	3	2	1	25	20	4	3	0	2	2	7	2	2	2	4	2	10	1	3	3	2	2	1	2	1	1
10 Chiang Rai	1	0	6	1	2	1	2	1	8	100	1	1	2	2	1	1	1	6	3	3	1	63	1	11	1	5	2	1	2	11	11	1	2	2	5	1	1	2	2	1
11 Chonburi	2	0	17	2	14	4	3	12	1	2	100	5	0	3	4	0	4	6	3	3	4	6	2	11	7	5	7	3	3	4	2	4	2	2	5	0	4	8	5	3
12 Chumphon	0	1	14	1	0	1	1	1	1	2	2	100	0	0	1	6	4	1	1	3	1	2	1	1	7	1	7	2	5	2	1	2	1	1	0	0	1	2	3	1
13 Kalasin	0	1	6	2	1	1	3	0	1	3	1	1	100	0	1	12	1	1	1	4	1	2	21	6	1	1	4	3	4	5	3	0	16	7	1	0	1	4	1	1
14 Kampaeng Phet	1	1	8	2	2	2	1	2	2	2	1	1	0	100	2	1	1	3	2	2	2	2	1	1	1	1	0	1	4	1	1	1	1	1	1	1	1	2	1	1
15 Kanchanaburi	5	1	18	1	2	1	2	0	1	2	2	5	0	2	100	0	1	1	1	2	2	2	3	6	2	5	4	3	2	1	2	2	3	2	1	1	1	2	1	0
16 Khon Kaen	1	0	6	1	1	0	5	0	0	1	1	1	6	0	1	100	1	2	1	6	1	1	6	6	2	1	4	5	2	1	1	2	16	7	0	1	1	0	1	3
17 Krabi	0	0	12	1	2	1	1	1	1	1	2	4	0	0	1	1	100	1	1	1	1	1	1	0	1	1	0	3	1	5	1	3	1	0	1	1	1	1	10	14
18 Lampang	0	1	8	1	1	0	1	1	1	5	1	1	1	3	1	2	2	100	14	2	1	1	1	1	0	0	0	1	1	1	3	1	1	1	1	1	1	2	0	0
19 Lamphun	0	1	5	1	1	1	1	1	11	4	1	1	1	3	2	1	1	9	100	2	1	1	1	1	3	3	1	1	2	1	9	2	0	0	1	0	1	1	1	2
20 Loei	1	0	10	2	2	1	3	0	4	3	3	0	3	2	0	10	0	2	1	100	2	2	2	5	0	0	6	1	5	0	3	0	6	3	0	1	2	1	0	0
21 Lopburi	0	1	12	2	3	2	2	0	0	1	4	2	1	1	2	1	1	4	4	1	100	1	1	2	7	4	1	6	1	2	2	3	1	1	2	1	0	2	1	0
22 Mae Hong Son	0	0	7	1	1	0	1	0	63	6	2	0	1	2	1	2	2	6	7	1	1	100	1	0	0	0	2	1	2	1	2	1	1	1	1	1	1	2	1	3
23 Maha Sarakham	1	1	6	4	1	0	3	0	2	1	2	0	10	1	1	21	1	1	1	1	1	1	100	1	0	1	3	6	1	1	1	2	1	0	1	0	1	2	0	0
24 Mukdahan	5	0	5	2	1	0	1	0	2	1	2	2	11	1	6	1	1	0	0	3	2	1	11	100	1	1	11	3	1	1	1	1	1	2	1	0	0	0	0	0
25 Nakhon Nayok	0	1	20	3	6	1	2	2	1	1	7	1	1	2	4	1	2	0	0	1	7	1	1	3	100	3	1	3	2	1	1	0	0	0	6	0	0	6	0	0
26 Nakhon Pathom	0	1	24	3	1	0	2	2	0	0	5	1	1	2	2	0	2	0	0	2	4	0	1	1	3	100	0	2	2	0	1	1	0	1	3	5	0	1	0	0
27 Nakhon Phanom	1	0	7	2	1	0	0	1	2	1	2	0	7	0	1	6	0	0	0	3	0	0	3	4	0	0	100	3	1	0	0	1	3	3	1	1	0	0	0	0
28 Nakhon Ratchasima	1	0	9	9	3	0	4	1	2	1	3	0	2	0	1	7	0	0	0	3	3	1	3	1	0	0	2	100	1	0	2	1	1	2	0	2	1	2	2	0
29 Nakhon Sawan	0	1	11	2	2	3	1	0	4	2	3	1	1	5	2	4	1	2	2	1	1	4	0	0	2	1	1	0	100	1	1	0	1	1	2	2	0	0	0	0
30 Nakhon Si Thammarat	0	0	12	1	1	0	1	0	2	1	4	2	3	0	1	1	2	5	1	1	0	1	1	0	0	0	0	0	2	100	1	1	1	1	2	2	2	0	2	5
31 Nan	0	0	7	1	1	0	1	0	10	11	2	0	1	2	0	6	1	6	3	0	3	2	1	1	1	1	3	1	1	0	100	0	1	3	0	0	0	1	0	0
32 Narathiwat	0	0	12	1	2	1	2	0	1	1	2	4	0	2	2	2	2	1	1	1	0	1	3	3	1	4	0	0	0	2	0	100	0	1	0	0	9	1	1	2
33 Nong Bua Lamphu	1	0	7	2	2	0	3	0	3	2	2	0	4	0	1	16	0	1	1	7	0	0	3	1	0	0	1	2	1	1	1	0	100	6	1	1	0	1	0	0
34 Nong Khai	1	0	6	2	1	0	2	0	3	2	2	0	4	1	1	7	0	1	1	1	3	0	2	1	0	0	3	3	1	1	2	0	3	100	1	1	0	0	0	0
35 Nonthaburi	0	1	35	1	1	3	1	0	2	1	5	0	1	1	2	0	1	1	2	0	1	0	3	2	1	9	3	3	2	1	0	0	1	0	100	7	0	1	0	1
36 Pathum Thani	0	1	33	3	3	1	0	2	2	5	0	1	1	2	2	0	1	3	1	3	3	1	0	0	1	4	3	3	1	0	0	0	0	1	4	100	0	0	1	1
37 Pattani	0	0	9	1	2	1	0	2	1	1	4	5	4	1	1	0	1	0	1	2	2	1	1	0	1	1	1	3	2	2	1	4	11	3	0	0	100	1	0	2
38 Phachinburi	0	0	16	4	11	1	1	2	1	2	8	2	1	1	4	0	1	1	1	2	2	0	2	0	2	2	1	1	1	2	1	0	1	1	2	3	2	100	0	1
39 Phangnga	0	0	14	1	3	0	1	1	2	1	5	3	1	1	1	2	6	1	1	2	1	0	1	0	0	2	1	3	2	10	0	1	0	1	1	1	2	1	100	2
40 Phatthalung	0	0	9	1	2	0	1	0	1	1	3	1	1	1	1	3	3	1	1	0	1	0	0	0	2	1	0	0	0	5	2	2	0	0	0	0	2	0	1	100

Extracted Province

Extracted Province

Province	1Annat Charoen	2Ang Thong	3Bangkok	4Buriram	5Chachoengsao	6Chainat	7Chaiyaphum	8Chanthaburi	9Chiang Mai	10Chiang Rai	11Chonburi	12Chumphon	13Kalasin	14Kampaeng Phet	15Kanchanaburi	16Khon Kaen	17Krabi	18Lampang	19Lamphun	20Loei	21Lopburi	22Mae Hong Son	23Maha Sarakham	24Mukdahan	25Nakhon Nayok	26Nakhon Pathom	27Nakhon Phanom	28Nakhon Ratchasima	29Nakhon Sawan	30Nakhon Si Thammarat	31Nan	32Narathiwat	33Nong Bua Lamphu	34Nong Khai	35Nonthaburi	36Pathum Thani	37Pattani	38Phachinburi	39Phangnga	40Phatthalung
76Yasothon	12	0	5	3	1	0	1	0	2	1	2	0	7	1	1	6	0	1	1	1	0	4	5	0	1	4	4	1	1	1	0	1	0	2	1	1	0	0	0	0
75Yala	0	0	10	1	2	0	1	0	1	1	4	1	1	1	2	1	1	1	0	1	0	1	0	1	0	2	1	4	0	21	0	1	1	2	12	1	1	0	1	2
74Uttaradit	0	0	7	1	1	0	2	0	8	4	2	0	2	2	1	4	0	6	4	4	1	1	1	0	0	3	1	1	3	2	1	5	0	1	2	1	0	0	0	0
73Uthai Thani	0	1	14	2	2	4	2	1	4	2	4	1	1	6	8	3	0	2	2	1	3	1	0	0	3	1	4	12	1	1	0	1	1	2	3	0	0	1	0	0
72Udon Thani	1	0	5	2	1	0	2	0	3	2	2	0	6	1	1	11	0	1	1	3	0	1	0	3	0	1	4	3	1	1	0	5	18	1	1	1	0	0	0	0
71Ubon Ratchathani	5	0	5	3	1	1	0	0	2	1	2	0	3	1	4	4	0	1	1	1	0	2	2	0	0	3	4	1	1	2	0	1	0	1	0	0	0	0	0	0
70Trang	0	0	11	1	2	0	1	0	1	1	4	1	1	1	1	2	4	1	1	0	1	0	0	1	0	1	0	2	1	15	0	2	0	1	2	2	1	0	1	14
69Trad	1	0	16	3	5	0	1	6	2	1	10	1	1	1	3	1	1	1	1	0	1	0	0	2	1	5	1	2	1	1	1	1	2	1	1	0	1	0	0	1
68Tak	0	0	12	1	2	0	2	0	9	3	3	0	1	8	3	3	0	5	5	1	2	1	0	0	2	1	3	4	1	1	0	1	1	2	0	1	1	0	0	0
67Surin	1	0	7	12	2	0	2	1	2	1	3	0	3	1	0	6	0	1	1	1	0	4	1	0	1	2	7	1	1	0	1	1	2	1	0	1	1	0	0	0
66Surat Thani	0	0	10	1	2	1	0	2	1	4	4	1	0	1	2	5	1	1	0	1	0	0	0	1	0	2	1	2	1	16	0	1	1	0	1	2	1	0	4	2
65Suphanburi	0	2	20	2	3	3	2	1	3	1	4	1	1	2	6	3	0	1	1	3	1	0	0	0	5	5	1	4	4	1	1	1	3	4	0	1	0	0	0	0
64Sukhothai	0	0	8	1	1	1	2	0	10	3	2	1	0	5	1	4	0	6	5	2	1	1	0	1	1	3	3	1	4	2	1	1	1	1	0	1	0	0	0	0
63Songkhla	0	0	7	1	2	0	1	0	1	3	1	1	0	1	2	1	1	0	1	0	0	0	1	0	2	1	6	0	4	0	1	1	2	1	5	0	1	0	1	5
62Singburi	0	3	13	1	2	4	2	0	3	1	4	0	1	2	2	3	0	1	1	6	1	0	1	0	3	1	4	5	1	1	0	1	2	3	3	0	0	0	0	0
61Si Saket	2	0	7	5	2	0	1	2	1	3	0	3	1	1	4	1	1	1	0	3	1	0	1	2	5	1	1	0	1	1	1	0	1	1	0	0	0	0	0	0
60Satun	0	0	11	1	2	0	1	0	1	4	1	1	0	4	2	2	0	1	1	0	1	0	1	0	2	1	7	0	3	0	1	1	2	3	1	0	1	0	0	6
59Saraburi	0	1	15	2	3	1	2	1	4	4	1	1	3	1	1	6	0	1	1	5	2	1	2	5	1	0	1	2	2	5	0	1	2	2	5	0	1	0	0	0
58Samut Songkham	0	1	18	2	3	1	2	1	6	1	1	1	2	1	1	6	1	1	0	0	6	1	4	2	2	1	1	0	1	2	3	1	0	1	0	0	0	1	0	1
57Samut Sakhon	0	0	25	1	3	0	1	0	2	1	6	1	1	1	2	2	0	1	1	0	1	0	6	1	3	1	2	1	0	0	1	4	4	0	1	0	0	0	0	1
56Samut Prakarn	0	0	41	1	4	0	1	1	2	1	7	0	1	1	2	2	0	1	1	0	1	0	3	0	3	1	1	0	0	0	1	6	1	3	5	0	0	0	0	0
55Sakon Nakhon	1	0	5	2	1	0	2	0	2	1	2	0	11	1	1	7	0	1	2	1	0	0	3	3	0	1	19	3	2	1	1	0	2	6	1	1	0	0	0	0
54Sa Kaeo	1	0	14	6	7	0	2	3	2	1	8	1	2	1	1	4	0	1	1	2	1	1	2	0	2	1	1	12	2	2	1	1	1	2	1	0	4	0	0	0
53Roi Et	3	0	5	4	1	0	2	0	1	2	0	1	11	1	9	0	0	1	1	2	1	1	10	3	0	1	3	5	1	2	1	0	0	1	1	2	1	0	0	0
52Rayong	0	0	21	2	7	0	1	2	2	1	18	1	1	1	1	3	1	1	2	0	3	1	4	2	1	1	0	2	4	1	1	0	1	2	3	1	1	0	0	1
51Ratchaburi	0	1	18	1	3	1	1	3	2	5	1	1	4	3	1	1	2	0	0	6	1	3	2	2	1	1	2	3	1	1	0	1	2	3	1	1	0	1	0	1
50Ranong	0	0	14	1	3	0	1	1	2	2	5	16	1	1	2	2	1	1	3	7	0	1	1	2	1	1	2	1	1	2	1	0	0	1	1	0	1	2	1	1
49Prachuap Khilikhan	0	0	12	1	3	0	1	3	1	5	2	1	1	2	1	1	0	1	1	0	2	0	1	0	2	3	1	4	1	1	0	1	1	2	1	1	0	1	1	1
48Phuket	0	0	3	1	1	0	0	1	1	2	0	0	0	6	0	0	0	0	0	0	0	0	0	0	1	0	0	0	0	10	0	3	0	0	3	0	0	3	4	3
47Phrae	0	0	5	1	1	0	1	0	14	6	2	0	2	1	0	22	6	2	2	1	6	2	1	1	0	0	1	2	1	1	6	1	1	2	1	1	0	1	0	0
46Phra Nakhon Si Ayudhya	0	1	19	1	3	1	0	2	4	1	2	0	1	1	3	1	0	4	3	2	1	0	1	0	3	7	1	0	1	1	0	1	1	3	1	1	0	0	0	0
45Phitsanulok	0	0	8	2	1	1	3	0	6	3	2	2	0	4	1	5	0	3	3	5	0	1	1	0	2	4	4	1	2	1	1	1	0	0	0	0	0	0	0	0
44Phichit	0	1	12	2	2	1	3	0	4	2	3	0	2	6	2	5	0	2	2	1	1	1	2	3	1	0	1	1	2	1	1	1	0	11	1	1	0	1	0	0
43Phetchaburi	0	0	17	2	3	2	1	3	3	6	1	2	3	3	0	4	4	2	3	1	1	2	3	1	1	0	1	1	2	1	1	1	0	1	1	2	0	1	0	1
42Phetchabun	0	0	12	2	2	0	9	3	2	3	8	0	2	2	2	3	4	1	1	2	7	4	1	2	2	1	1	2	3	1	1	1	0	1	1	2	0	1	0	0
41Phayao	0	0	6	1	1	0	1	0	13	24	2	2	0	1	1	3	0	6	4	1	6	4	2	1	1	1	1	2	1	1	10	1	2	1	1	1	0	0	0	0

	41Phayao	42Phetchabun	43Phetchaburi	44Phichit	45Phitsanulok	46Phra Nakhon Si Ayudhya	47Phrae	48Phuket	49Prachuap Khilikhan	50Ranong	51Ratchaburi	52Rayong	53Roi Et	54Sa Kaeo	55Sakon Nakhon	56Samut Prakarn	57Samut Sakhon	58Samut Songkham	59Saraburi	60Satun	61Si Saket	62Singburi	63Songkhla	64Sukhothai	65Suphanburi	66Surat Thani	67Surin	68Tak	69Trad	70Trang	71Ubon Ratchathani	72Udon Thani	73Uthai Thani	74Uttaradit	75Yala	76Yasothon
40Phatthalung	0	1	1	0	1	2	0	2	1	0	1	3	1	0	1	4	3	0	1	4	1	0	24	0	1	5	1	0	1	11	1	0	0	0	2	0
39Phangnga	0	1	1	0	1	3	0	6	2	1	2	4	1	1	6	3	0	1	1	1	5	1	1	1	1	20	1	1	2	2	1	0	0	1	0	0
38Phachinburi	1	2	1	1	5	1	0	1	0	1	5	2	3	1	6	3	0	4	0	2	0	1	1	2	1	2	1	0	1	2	0	0	1	0	1	0
37Pattani	0	1	1	0	1	2	0	1	0	1	3	1	0	1	4	2	0	2	1	0	0	1	20	0	1	3	1	0	1	1	1	0	0	0	10	0
36Pathum Thani	0	1	1	1	1	13	0	1	0	1	2	1	4	1	1	0	1	5	10	0	0	4	0	1	0	1	1	1	1	1	1	0	0	0	0	0
35Nonthaburi	0	1	1	1	1	9	0	1	0	1	2	3	1	1	1	9	7	1	3	0	0	1	1	2	1	1	1	1	0	0	0	1	0	0	0	0
34Nong Khai	1	2	0	1	2	2	1	0	0	0	1	2	2	1	7	3	1	0	1	0	2	0	2	1	1	1	1	0	0	2	1	32	0	1	0	1
33Nong Bua Lamphu	1	3	0	1	2	2	1	0	0	0	2	2	3	0	4	3	1	0	2	0	1	0	1	1	2	1	0	0	0	2	1	23	0	1	0	1
32Narathiwat	0	1	1	0	2	2	0	1	0	1	2	5	3	2	5	3	0	2	1	0	2	0	13	0	1	3	1	0	1	1	1	0	0	0	16	0
31Nan	11	2	0	1	3	2	6	0	1	0	2	4	1	2	3	2	1	0	1	0	1	0	2	4	1	1	1	1	0	2	4	2	0	4	0	1
30Nakhon Si Thammarat	0	1	1	0	1	4	0	3	2	1	2	4	1	0	1	6	3	0	2	2	1	0	11	0	1	13	1	1	1	4	2	1	0	2	0	0
29Nakhon Sawan	1	4	0	5	4	5	1	0	1	0	1	2	1	0	4	3	0	3	0	1	1	2	1	4	1	1	2	0	0	3	2	2	1	0	0	1
28Nakhon Ratchasima	1	2	0	1	2	3	1	0	1	0	3	3	1	2	4	2	0	3	0	3	0	1	1	0	1	1	4	1	0	3	3	1	0	1	0	1
27Nakhon Phanom	1	1	0	1	2	2	0	0	0	1	2	4	24	3	1	0	1	0	2	0	1	1	1	2	1	1	0	0	0	4	7	0	0	1	0	1
26Nakhon Pathom	0	1	1	1	1	9	1	1	0	1	3	4	1	0	1	9	10	0	3	0	0	1	1	0	2	1	1	1	0	2	2	0	1	0	0	0
25Nakhon Nayok	1	2	0	1	2	7	1	0	1	0	2	4	2	2	1	7	3	10	0	2	1	1	1	1	2	2	1	1	0	2	2	1	1	1	0	0
24Mukdahan	1	1	0	0	1	2	1	0	0	1	2	9	0	8	2	1	0	1	4	0	1	1	3	0	0	0	8	5	1	1	1	0	0	0	2	4
23Maha Sarakham	1	2	0	1	1	2	1	0	0	1	2	2	13	1	4	2	1	0	1	0	3	0	1	1	1	1	4	1	0	0	4	6	0	1	0	2
22Mae Hong Son	2	1	0	2	2	2	1	0	1	0	2	1	0	1	3	2	0	1	0	2	1	1	1	2	1	1	2	0	0	2	2	2	1	1	0	1
21Lopburi	1	3	1	2	2	9	1	0	0	1	3	1	0	1	5	3	0	1	9	1	1	1	1	1	1	2	1	0	2	1	0	0	0	0	0	0
20Loei	1	4	0	2	6	3	2	0	0	1	2	2	0	3	2	0	2	0	2	0	2	1	1	1	1	1	1	0	0	2	1	10	0	3	0	1
19Lamphun	2	1	0	1	2	3	3	0	1	0	2	1	1	0	0	2	1	0	1	0	1	1	2	1	0	1	2	3	0	0	1	2	0	2	0	0
18Lampang	4	2	1	1	3	4	10	0	1	0	2	1	0	2	0	2	0	1	0	1	3	1	1	3	0	0	2	2	0	3	1	0	3	1	0	0
17Krabi	0	1	1	0	2	2	0	6	2	1	4	1	0	1	5	3	0	1	2	1	0	0	1	0	7	13	1	1	1	4	1	0	0	1	0	0
16Khon Kaen	1	2	0	1	2	2	1	0	1	0	2	4	0	3	2	1	0	2	0	2	1	1	1	0	2	1	0	3	8	0	0	1	0	0	0	1
15Kanchanaburi	1	2	1	1	2	10	1	1	2	0	5	4	1	0	1	8	6	0	4	0	1	0	1	2	1	4	1	1	2	1	0	2	2	2	1	0
14Kamphaeng Phet	1	3	1	5	6	3	2	0	1	0	2	1	0	1	3	2	0	2	1	0	1	0	1	5	1	1	1	8	0	0	2	2	2	1	0	0
13Kalasin	1	1	0	1	1	2	1	0	1	0	2	2	10	0	10	2	0	1	0	3	0	1	1	0	1	1	3	1	0	0	4	9	0	1	0	2
12Chumphon	0	1	1	1	1	3	0	1	4	7	2	5	1	0	1	0	0	1	0	4	1	1	1	0	1	10	1	1	0	1	2	2	0	0	1	0
11Chonburi	0	1	1	1	1	4	1	1	2	0	1	16	1	1	1	8	4	0	1	0	0	1	2	1	1	1	0	0	2	1	0	2	1	0	0	1
10Chiang Rai	11	1	0	1	2	2	3	0	1	0	1	2	1	0	1	0	0	1	0	0	1	1	1	2	0	1	1	2	0	1	1	2	0	2	0	0
9Chiang Mai	3	1	0	2	2	3	3	0	0	1	1	2	1	0	1	0	0	1	0	1	1	2	1	1	1	2	0	1	0	2	0	0	2	1	0	0
8Chanthaburi	1	1	1	1	1	3	1	1	2	0	1	17	2	3	1	6	3	0	2	0	3	0	2	1	1	2	3	1	7	0	3	0	1	1	0	1
7Chaiyaphum	1	10	0	2	3	3	1	0	1	1	2	1	3	1	2	3	0	2	0	2	0	1	1	1	2	1	1	1	0	3	5	1	0	0	1	1
6Chainat	1	3	1	2	2	7	1	0	0	2	3	1	1	0	3	1	0	3	0	1	1	6	1	1	6	1	1	2	0	0	2	2	4	0	0	0
5Chachoengsao	0	1	1	1	5	1	1	0	0	1	3	9	1	1	1	8	4	0	3	0	0	1	2	1	2	1	0	0	1	0	2	1	0	1	0	1
4Buriram	0	2	0	1	3	3	1	0	0	1	2	4	2	2	0	5	0	0	2	0	5	1	1	1	1	1	13	1	0	0	5	1	0	0	1	1
3Bangkok	1	0	1	1	1	5	1	0	1	1	2	14	1	1	1	4	5	0	2	0	1	1	1	1	1	1	1	1	1	1	1	1	0	0	0	1
2Ang Thong	1	2	0	1	2	22	0	0	1	0	1	2	3	1	0	1	0	0	6	0	0	4	0	1	6	1	1	1	1	1	1	2	2	1	1	0
1Amnat Charoen	0	1	0	0	1	1	0	0	0	0	2	0	10	0	4	2	1	0	1	0	8	0	1	1	0	0	4	0	1	0	22	3	0	1	0	12

Extracted Province

Chapter 2 Evaluating the Spatial Linkages of Thailand's Inter-Provincial Economies and Industries: An Input-Output Approach 31

Extracted Province

Province	41	42	43	44	45	46	47	48	49	50	51	52	53	54	55	56	57	58	59	60	61	62	63	64	65	66	67	68	69	70	71	72	73	74	75	76
76Yasothon	0	1	0	0	1	1	0	0	0	0	1	2	20	0	4	2	1	0	1	0	7	0	1	0	0	1	5	0	0	0	12	4	0	0	1	100
75Yala	0	1	1	0	1	2	0	1	0	1	3	1	0	1	4	2	0	1	2	1	0	0	19	0	1	3	1	0	1	1	3	1	0	0	100	0
74Uttaradit	2	3	0	2	10	3	9	0	1	0	2	1	0	2	3	2	0	1	0	1	1	5	1	1	3	2	0	0	2	4	0	0	2	100	0	0
73Uthai Thani	1	3	1	3	3	5	1	0	1	0	2	3	1	1	5	3	0	2	0	1	2	4	1	3	1	0	2	2	0	0	2	2	100	0	0	0
72Udon Thani	1	2	0	0	2	1	1	0	0	0	0	1	3	1	8	2	1	0	2	0	1	1	0	1	0	1	2	1	0	0	2	100	0	1	0	1
71Ubon Ratchathani	0	1	0	0	1	2	0	0	1	0	1	2	5	1	3	2	1	0	1	0	16	1	0	0	1	5	0	1	0	0	100	3	1	0	1	3
70Trang	0	1	1	0	1	2	0	2	1	1	3	1	0	1	5	3	0	0	4	1	0	15	0	1	6	1	0	1	0	100	1	1	0	2	0	1
69Trad	0	1	1	0	1	3	1	1	2	0	1	11	2	2	1	7	3	0	2	0	2	1	1	2	2	1	1	2	100	3	2	0	1	1	1	1
68Tak	1	2	1	2	4	5	2	1	0	2	3	1	2	0	1	5	3	0	3	0	3	1	0	16	1	0	1	100	0	0	2	2	1	2	0	0
67Surin	0	1	0	1	1	2	0	0	1	0	3	7	1	2	3	2	1	0	1	0	16	1	1	0	1	1	100	1	1	0	8	3	0	1	0	2
66Surat Thani	0	1	0	1	1	2	0	3	2	2	4	1	0	1	4	3	0	1	1	1	0	6	0	1	1	100	1	1	1	2	1	1	0	1	0	0
65Suphanburi	1	2	1	2	2	11	1	0	1	0	3	3	1	1	7	5	4	0	1	2	1	2	1	1	100	1	1	2	2	2	1	0	0	2	2	0
64Sukhothai	2	3	0	2	9	3	4	0	1	0	1	2	1	0	1	3	2	0	1	1	0	1	0	100	1	1	5	0	0	2	1	3	1	5	0	0
63Songkhla	0	1	0	0	1	2	0	1	0	1	3	1	0	1	3	2	0	1	5	1	0	0	100	0	0	4	1	0	1	2	1	1	0	0	4	0
62Singburi	1	2	1	2	2	11	1	0	1	0	3	1	0	1	6	3	0	5	0	1	0	100	1	1	4	1	0	0	1	2	1	1	0	0	0	0
61Si Saket	0	1	0	0	1	2	0	0	1	0	1	2	6	1	2	3	1	0	1	0	100	0	1	1	1	1	13	0	1	0	23	3	0	0	0	2
60Satun	0	1	0	0	1	2	0	2	0	1	4	1	0	1	5	3	0	1	1	100	1	1	31	0	1	4	1	0	4	1	1	0	0	3	0	0
59Saraburi	0	1	1	1	1	14	0	1	0	1	3	1	1	7	4	1	1	0	100	1	1	1	0	1	7	1	1	2	2	1	1	0	1	0	0	0
58Samut Songkham	1	1	5	1	1	4	1	1	3	0	11	4	1	1	7	13	2	100	2	1	0	2	1	2	2	1	1	0	2	2	1	1	1	1	1	1
57Samut Sakhon	0	1	1	1	1	6	1	1	0	3	4	1	0	1	1	11	100	2	1	0	1	0	1	1	1	1	0	0	1	1	0	0	0	0	0	0
56Samut Prakarn	0	1	1	0	1	5	0	1	0	1	4	0	1	1	2	100	6	0	2	0	1	0	1	1	2	1	0	0	2	1	0	0	0	1	0	0
55Sakon Nakhon	1	1	0	1	1	1	1	0	0	0	1	2	4	0	100	2	1	0	1	0	2	0	1	1	0	1	2	1	0	0	4	14	0	1	0	1
54Sa Kaeo	1	2	1	1	1	3	1	0	1	0	1	7	2	100	2	6	3	0	2	0	3	0	2	1	1	0	4	1	2	0	3	2	0	1	0	1
53Roi Et	0	1	0	1	1	2	1	0	0	0	1	2	100	4	2	1	0	1	0	6	0	1	0	1	6	0	0	0	7	5	0	1	0	0	0	6
52Rayong	1	1	1	1	6	1	1	2	0	2	2	100	5	0	3	11	2	1	2	2	1	0	2	2	1	2	0	2	2	1	1	1	1	1	1	1
51Ratchaburi	1	1	5	1	2	6	1	1	3	0	100	4	1	1	7	8	2	2	1	0	1	3	2	1	3	2	1	2	2	1	2	2	1	1	1	1
50Ranong	0	1	1	1	1	3	0	2	3	100	2	5	1	1	6	3	0	2	1	1	0	4	1	1	14	1	1	1	1	2	1	0	0	1	1	0
49Prachuap Khilikhan	1	1	2	1	1	4	1	1	100	2	5	1	1	5	4	0	2	1	1	0	4	1	1	4	1	1	1	2	1	1	2	2	1	1	1	1
48Phuket	0	0	0	0	0	1	0	100	1	1	0	1	0	1	1	0	0	2	1	0	8	0	0	8	1	0	3	1	0	0	2	0	0	0	2	0
47Phrae	4	2	0	0	4	2	100	0	0	0	1	1	0	0	2	1	0	1	1	0	1	1	0	4	1	1	2	0	0	1	1	9	0	9	0	0
46Phra Nakhon Si Ayudhya	0	1	1	1	4	100	0	0	1	1	1	1	1	3	1	0	6	0	1	0	1	1	1	1	6	1	1	2	1	1	1	1	0	0	0	0
45Phitsanulok	1	1	6	0	100	3	3	0	0	1	2	1	0	2	3	2	0	0	1	0	2	1	0	6	1	1	2	1	0	0	2	4	7	0	0	0
44Phichit	1	7	1	100	9	5	1	0	1	0	1	3	1	0	1	5	3	0	3	0	1	1	0	3	1	1	2	1	0	2	2	3	1	2	0	0
43Phetchaburi	1	1	100	1	1	4	1	1	8	1	10	5	1	1	7	6	1	2	2	1	0	3	1	2	2	1	1	1	0	1	2	2	1	1	0	0
42Phetchabun	1	100	1	7	7	1	0	0	0	0	3	2	1	2	5	3	0	3	1	2	1	1	2	2	3	0	2	1	0	0	2	4	2	2	0	1
41Phayao	100	1	0	1	2	2	4	0	1	0	1	2	1	0	1	3	1	0	1	0	1	0	0	2	1	3	1	0	0	0	1	3	0	2	2	0

Table 4 : Percentage Decrease in Production When Provinces in Thailand are Eliminated

Extracted Province	1Agriculture	2Mining and Quarrying	3Food Manufacturing	4Textile Industry	5Saw Mills and Wood Products	6Paper and Paper Products	7Printing and Publishing	8Chemical Industries	9Petroleum Refineries	10Rubber and Plastic Products	11Non-metallic Products	12Basic Metal	13Fabricated Metal Products	14Electrical Machinery and Apparatus	15Industrial Machinery	16Motor Vehcile	17Other Transportation Equipment	18Other Manufacturing Products	19Electricity and Water Works	20Construction	21Trade and Transport, Communication	22Accomodation and food service activities	23Banking and Insurance	24Other Services
1Amnat Charoen	1	0	0	0	0	1	1	0	0	0	0	0	0	0	0	0	0	0	1	0	1	0	1	1
2Ang Thong	1	1	0	0	0	1	1	1	1	0	1	1	0	1	1	0	1	0	1	1	1	0	1	1
3Bangkok	23	31	29	36	26	42	42	38	37	25	34	41	38	23	48	37	51	38	34	43	56	64	64	36
4Buriram	3	2	2	2	1	2	3	1	2	1	2	1	1	1	1	1	2	1	2	2	2	2	3	5
5Chachoengsao	5	6	7	11	5	12	13	12	8	6	7	11	9	5	8	6	11	11	6	4	3	1	5	4
6Chainat	1	1	0	0	0	1	1	1	1	0	1	0	0	0	1	0	1	0	1	1	1	1	1	2
7Chaiyaphum	3	1	2	1	1	2	2	1	2	1	1	1	1	1	1	1	1	1	2	1	2	2	2	4
8Chanthaburi	2	1	1	1	1	1	1	1	1	0	1	1	1	0	1	1	1	1	1	1	1	1	2	2
9Chiang Mai	4	3	3	2	4	4	4	2	3	1	4	2	3	2	4	3	4	2	4	5	4	5	4	8
10Chiang Rai	3	2	1	1	1	2	2	1	1	1	1	1	1	1	1	1	2	1	2	1	2	2	2	4
11Chonburi	9	14	12	17	9	19	22	20	13	10	12	18	15	9	15	12	20	18	18	9	8	9	10	7
12Chumphon	3	1	1	0	2	1	1	1	1	1	1	1	1	0	1	0	1	0	1	1	1	1	1	2
13Kalasin	3	3	2	2	1	3	3	2	2	1	1	2	1	1	1	1	2	2	2	1	2	2	2	4
14Kampaeng Phet	2	1	1	1	1	1	2	1	1	1	1	1	1	0	1	1	1	1	1	1	2	1	2	3
15Kanchanaburi	3	8	2	2	4	2	2	1	2	1	3	1	2	2	2	1	2	2	2	1	2	1	2	3
16Khon Kaen	5	4	5	4	4	4	4	2	4	2	5	3	4	3	3	2	3	3	4	3	4	3	4	8
17Krabi	3	1	1	0	1	1	1	1	1	1	1	1	1	0	1	0	1	0	1	1	1	1	1	2
18Lampang	2	4	1	1	2	2	2	1	1	1	2	1	1	1	1	1	1	1	2	2	2	1	2	3
19Lamphun	2	1	3	2	6	2	1	1	1	1	5	2	2	4	2	1	2	3	2	1	1	1	2	2
20Loei	3	1	1	1	1	1	1	1	1	0	1	0	1	0	1	1	1	1	1	1	1	1	1	2
21Lopburi	3	3	2	1	2	3	2	3	3	2	4	3	2	5	3	2	2	1	3	2	2	1	2	4
22Mae Hong Son	1	0	0	0	0	1	1	0	0	0	0	0	0	0	0	0	0	0	0	1	0	0	0	1
23Maha Sarakham	2	1	1	1	1	2	2	1	1	1	1	1	1	0	1	1	1	1	2	1	2	1	2	4
24Mukdahan	1	0	0	0	0	1	1	0	0	0	0	0	0	0	0	0	0	0	1	0	1	0	1	1
25Nakhon Nayok	1	0	0	0	0	1	1	0	1	0	0	0	0	0	0	0	0	0	1	0	1	1	1	1
26Nakhon Pathom	4	5	4	4	4	8	4	3	6	4	4	10	7	5	10	9	5	4	4	3	2	4	4	5
27Nakhon Phanom	2	1	1	1	1	1	2	1	1	0	1	0	1	0	1	1	1	1	1	1	1	1	1	3
28Nakhon Ratchasima	7	5	6	4	5	5	6	3	5	3	5	4	5	3	5	3	4	3	6	5	5	5	6	9
29Nakhon Sawan	4	2	2	2	3	2	3	2	2	1	3	1	2	2	2	1	2	2	2	2	2	2	3	4
30Nakhon Si Thammarat	6	9	2	2	5	3	3	4	3	5	3	2	2	1	3	2	3	2	5	3	3	2	3	5
31Nan	1	1	1	0	1	1	1	1	1	0	1	0	1	0	1	0	1	0	1	1	1	1	1	2
32Narathiwat	3	1	1	1	1	1	1	1	1	1	1	1	0	1	0	1	0	1	1	1	1	1	1	2
33Nong Bua Lamphu	1	1	1	1	0	1	1	0	1	0	0	0	0	0	0	0	1	0	1	1	1	1	1	1
34Nong Khai	2	1	1	1	1	1	2	1	1	1	1	1	1	0	1	1	1	1	1	1	2	1	2	3
35Nonthaburi	2	4	3	3	3	5	3	2	4	3	4	7	5	3	8	7	4	3	4	6	3	3	5	5
36Pathum Thani	4	7	5	6	6	10	4	4	8	6	7	14	10	7	15	14	7	5	7	8	3	3	5	5
37Pattani	3	1	1	1	1	1	1	1	1	1	1	0	1	0	1	1	1	1	1	1	1	1	1	2
38Phachinburi	3	2	1	1	1	2	2	2	2	1	1	1	1	1	1	1	2	1	2	1	2	2	2	3
39Phangnga	2	1	0	0	1	1	1	1	1	1	0	0	0	0	0	0	0	0	1	1	1	1	1	1
40Phatthalung	2	1	1	0	1	1	1	1	1	1	1	1	1	0	1	1	1	0	1	1	1	1	1	2

estimating the operational damage rates at sectoral and provincial levels, we can examine the resultant indirect spatial economic damages. In this analysis, the provincial order is based on statistical data. By using provincial proximity matrices and adjacency matrices, this allows us to link spatial econometric modeling.

References

Akiyama, Y. (1996), "An Analysis of the Decentralization Policy in Thailand with the Interregional Input-Output

	1Agriculture	2Mining and Quarrying	3Food Manufacturing	4Textile Industry	5Saw Mills and Wood Products	6Paper and Paper Products	7Printing and Publishing	8Chemical Industries	9Petroleum Refineries	10Rubber and Plastic Products	11Non-metallic Products	12Basic Metal	13Fabricated Metal Products	14Electrical Machinery and Apparatus	15Industrial Machinery	16Motor Vehcile	17Other Transportation Equipment	18Other Manufacturing Products	19Electricity and Water Works	20Construction	21Trade and Transport, Communication	22Accomodation and food service activities	23Banking and Insurance	24Other Services
41Phayao	1	1	1	1	1	1	1	1	1	0	1	0	1	0	1	0	1	1	1	1	1	1	1	2
42Phetchabun	4	2	1	1	1	2	2	1	2	1	1	1	1	1	1	1	1	1	2	1	2	1	2	4
43Phetchaburi	2	2	1	1	1	2	2	2	1	1	1	1	1	1	1	1	2	1	2	1	1	1	2	3
44Phichit	2	2	1	1	1	1	1	1	1	0	1	0	1	0	1	0	1	1	1	1	1	1	1	2
45Phitsanulok	3	1	1	1	2	2	2	1	2	1	2	1	1	1	2	1	2	1	2	2	2	1	2	4
46Phra Nakhon Si Ayudhya	5	12	6	6	9	13	3	18	17	11	23	19	12	34	16	13	5	6	8	3	4	2	6	5
47Phrae	1	1	1	1	1	1	1	1	1	0	1	1	1	0	1	1	1	1	1	1	1	1	1	2
48Phuket	2	1	1	0	1	1	1	1	1	1	1	1	1	0	2	1	1	0	1	1	1	6	1	1
49Prachuap Khilikhan	2	2	2	3	2	4	4	4	3	2	2	3	3	2	3	2	4	3	2	1	2	1	2	2
50Ranong	1	0	0	0	1	0	0	0	0	0	0	0	0	0	0	0	0	0	0	0	0	0	1	1
51Ratchaburi	4	5	2	3	2	4	4	4	3	2	2	3	3	1	3	2	4	3	11	2	2	1	3	4
52Rayong	8	71	11	17	8	17	21	19	13	10	10	16	13	8	13	10	19	18	16	4	4	2	7	5
53Roi Et	3	2	2	1	1	2	2	1	2	1	1	1	1	1	1	1	1	1	2	1	2	2	2	4
54Sa Kaeo	2	1	1	1	1	1	1	1	1	0	1	1	1	0	1	1	1	1	1	1	1	1	1	2
55Sakon Nakhon	2	1	1	1	1	2	2	1	2	1	1	1	1	1	1	1	1	1	2	1	2	1	2	4
56Samut Prakarn	10	18	17	19	14	28	9	10	24	19	16	38	28	21	39	40	19	16	15	9	6	5	12	6
57Samut Sakhon	6	9	9	10	7	15	4	5	12	10	8	20	14	12	22	23	10	8	6	3	3	1	5	3
58Samut Songkham	1	0	0	0	0	1	1	0	1	0	0	0	0	0	0	0	1	0	1	0	1	0	1	1
59Saraburi	3	8	2	2	3	5	2	7	6	4	8	7	4	13	6	5	2	2	5	2	2	1	3	3
60Satun	2	1	1	0	1	1	1	1	1	1	1	0	0	0	0	0	0	0	1	0	1	0	1	1
61Si Saket	3	2	2	1	1	2	2	1	2	1	1	1	0	1	1	2	1	2	1	2	2	2	2	4
62Singburi	1	1	0	0	0	1	1	1	1	0	1	1	1	1	0	0	0	1	0	1	0	1	1	1
63Songkhla	8	3	4	2	13	4	3	8	3	13	5	3	3	1	4	2	3	2	4	3	3	3	4	6
64Sukhothai	2	1	1	1	1	1	1	1	1	0	1	0	1	0	1	1	1	1	1	1	1	1	1	2
65Suphanburi	3	3	1	1	1	2	2	2	2	1	1	1	1	1	1	1	2	1	2	1	2	1	2	3
66Surat Thani	7	3	2	1	6	2	2	4	2	6	3	2	2	1	2	1	2	1	3	2	2	4	3	4
67Surin	3	2	2	1	1	2	2	1	2	1	1	1	1	1	1	1	1	2	1	2	2	2	2	4
68Tak	2	2	1	1	1	1	1	1	1	0	1	1	1	1	1	1	1	1	1	1	1	1	1	2
69Trad	5	1	1	1	3	1	1	2	1	3	1	1	1	0	1	0	1	1	1	1	1	1	1	2
70Trang	1	1	0	0	0	1	1	0	1	0	1	0	0	0	0	1	0	1	1	1	1	1	1	2
71Ubon Ratchathani	3	2	2	2	2	3	3	2	2	1	2	1	2	1	2	1	2	2	3	2	3	2	3	5
72Udon Thani	3	2	2	2	2	3	3	2	2	1	2	2	2	1	2	2	2	2	3	3	3	2	3	5
73Uthai Thani	1	1	0	0	0	1	1	0	1	0	0	0	0	0	0	0	1	0	1	1	1	0	1	1
74Uttaradit	2	1	1	1	1	1	1	1	1	0	1	0	1	1	1	0	1	1	1	1	1	1	1	2
75Yala	3	1	1	0	1	1	1	1	1	1	1	0	1	0	1	0	1	0	1	1	1	1	1	2
76Yasothon	1	1	1	1	0	1	1	0	1	0	0	0	0	0	0	0	1	0	1	1	1	1	1	1

Table," *Input-Output Analysis,* 7(3), pp.17-23 (in Japanese).

Bunditsakulchai, P. (2016), "Review of the Potential for Constructing Inter-Regional Input-Output Table of Thailand and the Application for Transportation and Logistic Research," *Journal of Transportation and Logistics,* 9(1), pp.109-134.

Chenery, H. B. (1953), "Regional Analysis," Chenery, H. B., P. G. Clark, and V. C. Pinna (eds.), *The Structure and Growth of the Italian Economy,* U.S. Mutual Security Agency, Rome: USA.

Chintayarangsan, R. (1990), *Industrial Structure and Inter-Industry Linkages,* Thailand Development Research Institute, Foundation.

Dietzenbacher, E., and M. L. Lahr (2013), "Expanding Extractions," *Economic System Research,* 25(3), pp.341-360.

Isard, W. (1951), "Interregional and Regional Input-Output Analysis: A Model of a Space-Economy," *The Review of Economics and Statistics,* 33(4), pp.318-328.

Kumagai, S., T. Gokan, I. Isono, K. Hayakawa, K. Tsubato, and S. Keola (2013), *Geo-Economic Dataset for Asia,* IDE-JETRO.

Leontief, W., and A. Strout (1963), "Multiregional Input-Output Analysis," Barna, T. (ed.), *Structural Interdependence and Economic Development,* London: Macmillan (St. Martin's Press).

Miller, R., and P. D. Blair (2009), *Input-Output Analysis Foundations and Extensions,* Second Edition, Cambridge University Press.

Miller, R. E., and M. L. Lahr (2001), "A Taxonomy of Extractions," Lahr, M. L., and R. E. Miller (eds.), *Regional Science Perspectives in Economics: A Festschrift in Memory of Benjamin H. Stevens,* Amsterdam: Elsevier Science.

Ministry of Land, Infrastructure, Transport and Tourism, Japan (MLIT) (2017), Thailand, An Overview of Spatial Policy in Asian and European Countries (http://www.mlit.go.jp/kokudokeikaku/international/spw/general/thailand/index_e.html).

Moses, L. N. (1955), "The Stability of Interregional Trading Patterns and Input-Output Analysis," *American Economic Review,* 45(5), pp.803-832.

Nishimura, K. (2006), "Multiregional Input-Output Table with Cross Hauling: Estimation and Application to the China-Hanto Region," *The Journal of Economic Studies,* 33, pp.103-114 (in Japanese).

Shibusawa, H., I. Uchida, and I. Shimabukuro (2018), "Evaluating the Regional Economy and Industrial Structure Using IRIO and MRIO Tables for Municipalities in Aichi and Okinawa Prefectures," *Asia-Pacific Journal of Regional Science* (https:/doi.org/10.1007/s41685-018-0093-1).

Sim, B., F. Secretario, and E. Susan (2007), *Developing an Interregional Input-Output Table for Cross-Border Economies: An Application to Lao People's Democratic Republic and Thailand,* Asian Development Bank.

Unger, D., and C. Mahakanjana (2016), "Decentralization in. Thailand," *Journal of Southeast Asian Economies (JSEAE),* 33(2), pp.172-187.

Yamada, M., and Y. Owaki (2012), "Estimation of the Multiregional Input-Output Table for Four Regions in Aichi," *Chukyo University Institute of Economics,* Discussion Paper Series, 1205, pp.1-53 (in Japanese).

Chapter 3

Climate Changes and the Living Standards:
A Regional-Scale Assessment of the Vulnerability in Vietnam

Yosuke TAKEDA, Van NGHIEM, and Ichihiro UCHIDA

Abstract

This paper[1] addresses vulnerability to climate changes. It assesses the economic effects of climate changes on the living standards in a regional-scale of Vietnam. First, we arrange general concepts related to vulnerability in the climate change literature. Vulnerability to climate changes is a multidimensional continuum characterized by a function of exposure, sensitivity and adaptability. Second, we measure some dimensions of climate changes in Vietnam. Our assessment suggests that the exposures some regions face in Vietnam are lower temperature or less precipitation. Third, we tabulate proxies for the living standards, the income sources and the expenditure items in the Vietnamese regions. As results, we can identify the sectors and the regions which are vulnerable to the climate changes in a regional-scale of Vietnam.

JEL : Q54, R11, R22

Keywords : Climate Changes, Living Standards, Vulnerability, Externality

1. Introduction

As *the Stern Review* inspired us to recognize, climate changes have had very serious impacts on economic growth and development especially in developing countries. It is no exaggeration that the poverty reduction depends on adaptive capacity to the climate changes. Recently the World Bank reports that average household consumption in the South Asia declines after average temperature exceeds a peak and increases in rainfall are generally associated with higher living standards (Mani et al. 2018). The report shows that most of the 'hotspots' are in inland areas, instead of relatively richer coastal areas that previous analyses of climate change focused on.

This paper focuses on Vietnam, which is one of the countries heavily exposed to such climate changes as in temperature or rainfall (The World Bank 2010). The climate exposure stems not only from the socio-economic conditions largely depending on agriculture, forestry and fishery with no diversification of income sources due to climate-sensitive resource dependency. The exposure is also from geographical conditions of a one side of the nation bordering the South China Sea between two fertile rice-producing and populated areas of the Red River and the Mekong River Deltas. To what extent do the living standards of the Vietnamese suffer from the climate changes?

In order to explore the fundamental question, we take the following steps in this paper. First, we

---

1 We are grateful for helpful comments to the participants in the Center for China and Asian Studies International Workshop on "Japanese Companies Operating and Local Consumer Behavior in East Asia" on 9-10th of December 2017, Hanoi, Vietnam and a panel discussion at the conference "Individual Behavior, Climate Change, and Sustainability" (IBCCS) on 19th of July 2018, Hanoi, Vietnam.

arrange general concepts related to vulnerability in the climate change literature (O'Brien et al. 2004). Second, we measure some dimensions of climate changes in Vietnam, taking account of dependency of climate vulnerability on a scale of analysis (Gibson et al. 2000). Our assessment of climate changes is a regional-scale. Third, we tabulate proxies for the living standards, the income sources and the expenditure items in the Vietnamese regions.

Finally, we make qualitative conclusions on regional-scale assessment of the vulnerability in Vietnam, adding further analyses on household-level Engel curves to identify household attributes vulnerable to the climate changes.

2. Conceptualizing Vulnerability to Climate Changes and the Living Standards

First of all, we make clear our concepts on vulnerability to climate changes and the economic effects on the living standards. We then follow the climate impacts literature (for instance, O'Brien et al. 2004; Tol 2009; Fritzsche et al. 2014).

2. 1. Vulnerability / Resilience

Vulnerability is defined as the extent to which a system is susceptible to sustaining damages from climate changes. It is a biophysical and socioeconomic state or condition that is considered as a function of exposure, sensitivity, and adaptive capacity (Figure 1). Resilience is the opposite of vulnerability.

Exposure is the degree of climate stress on a particular unit of analysis. Climate stress is long-term changes in climate conditions or changes in climate variability or magnitude/frequency of extreme events. Typical factors of exposure are temperature and precipitation, directly linked to climate parameters determining vulnerability.

Sensitivity is also the degree of which a system will respond adversely or beneficially to a climate change exposure. Climate sensitivity is shaped not only by natural/ physical attributes of the system, but also by societal environment including human activities which affect the physical constitution of the system.

Exposure and sensitivity have in combination potential impacts of climate changes.

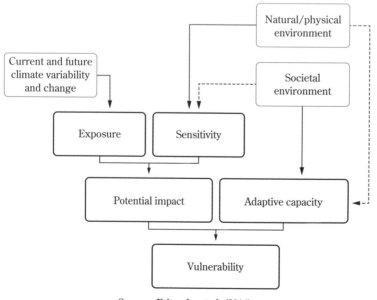

Source : Fritzsche et al. (2014)
Figure 1 : Components of Vulnerability

The potential impacts form a chain stretching from direct biophysical sphere to indirect societal sphere. For the developing countries like Vietnam where the economy largely depends on natural resources, the link between biophysical and societal impacts is particularly strong.

Adaptive capacity is the capacity of a system to adjust in response to actual or potential climate impacts. It is considered as a function of wealth, technology, education, information, skills, infrastructure, access to resources, and stability and management capabilities. Adaptability to climate changes is determined by the societal capacities fostered through nature-society interactions within conscious communities of multi-scale: country, region, corporation, social group or households.

Vulnerability is thus a multidimensional continuum characterized by a function of exposure, sensitivity and adaptability. It has three qualifications we should recognize. First, it is a differential concept that the applicability varies across physical space or societal environment. This paper applies the concept to the recent years in Vietnam. Second, the concept is scale-dependent, depending on a unit of analysis (Gibson et al. 2000; O'Brien et al. 2004) which in our paper, the scale of analysis is regions in social lives of the Vietnamese households. Finally, vulnerability is dynamically changing over time as the underlying structures evolve. Our analysis below should investigate in details the evolving structures in the Vietnamese society.

2. 2. Economic Effects of Climate Changes on the Living Standards

Climate change includes rising temperatures, changing precipitation patterns, and intensifying extreme events, such as storms and droughts. All these have profound repercussions for societies, from sudden economic disruptions to a longer-term decline in living standards. In this analysis, household consumption expenditures are used as a proxy for living standards.

Rising average temperatures can affect living standards through diverse pathways, such as agricultural and labor productivity, health, migration, and other factors that affect economic growth and poverty reduction (Figure 2).

They can dampen agricultural productivity, leading to a decline in living standards for agriculture-dependent households. A warmer climate can also increase the propagation of vector-borne and other infectious diseases, resulting in lost productivity and income. At the same time, a warmer climate can increase productivity in historically colder regions, such as mountainous areas. Days of extreme heat are generally correlated with lower worker productivity, especially in areas that

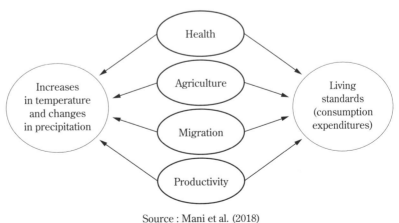

Source : Mani et al. (2018)
Figure 2 : Economic Effects of Climate Changes on the Living Standards

are already warm. A changing climate can force people out of their traditional professional domains, resulting in individuals not earning as much income. Previous research on climate change in South Asia and associated policy prescriptions has focused on disaster-resilient infrastructure and emergency responses, such as building

Climate changes themselves result from greenhouse-gas (GHG) emissions associated with economic activities including energy, industry, transport and land use. The science of climate change means that this is a very different form of externality from the types commonly analyzed. Climate change has special features that, together, pose particular challenges for the standard economic theory of externalities. There are four distinct issues that will be considered in turn in the sections below.

First, climate change is an externality that is global in both its causes and consequences. The incremental impact of a tone of GHG on climate change is independent of where in the world it is emitted, unlike other negative impacts such as air pollution and its cost to public health. It is because GHGs diffuse in the atmosphere and because local climatic changes depend on the global climate system. While different countries produce different volumes the marginal damage of an extra unit is independent of where it comes from in the world.

Second, the impacts of climate change are persistent and develop over time. Once in the atmosphere, some GHGs stay there for hundreds of years. Furthermore, the climate system is slow to respond to increases in atmospheric GHG concentrations and there are yet more lags in the environmental, economic and social response to climate change. The effects of GHGs are being experienced now and will continue to work their way through in the very long term.

Third, the uncertainties are considerable, both about the potential size, type and timing of impacts and about the costs of combating climate change; hence the framework used must be able to handle risk and uncertainty.

Fourth, the impacts are likely to have a significant effect on the global economy if action is not taken to prevent climate change, so the analysis has to consider potentially non-marginal changes to societies, not merely small changes amenable to ordinary project appraisal.

3. Measuring Climate Changes in Vietnam

In order to estimate economic effects of climate changes on the living standards, we take a statistical approach, instead of an enumerative method that estimates of the physical effects of climate change are obtained one by one from natural science papers based on some combination of climate models (Tol 2009).

Our statistical approach requires measurements of climate changes in Vietnam. We alternate some measures as an indicator of climate changes in Vietnam: the geographical characteristics, changes in climate seasonality, trends in temperature and rainfall, and changes in regional climate.

3. 1. Geographical Characteristics

Vietnam is one of the countries most affected by natural disasters and climate changes. Storms and floods are the most frequent and severe natural disasters affecting Vietnam. The country is suffering 6 to 7 typhoons on average every year. Between 1990 and 2010, 74 floods have occurred in the river systems. Severe drought, saline water intrusion, landslides and other natural disasters are hindering the development. Extreme disasters are more frequent in recent years, causing more damage to people and impacting significantly on the economy (UNDP 2015).

Vietnam consists of 8 regions: Northeast, Northwest, Red River Delta, North Central Coast, South Central Coast, Central Highlands, Southeast, and Mekong River Delta (Figure 3). Since 2006, the Government has arranged into 6 regions which are: North-midland and mountain areas, Red River Delta, North Central and Central Coastal areas, Central Highlands, Southeast, and Mekong River Delta.

Each region exposes geographical features. Huge number of people are densely populated at the capital Hanoi, Red River Delta or Ho Chi Minh City, and other big provinces near Mekong River Delta. Each of the populated cities along Red River or Mekong River is fertile rice-growing area, but historically prone to river flooding. The long coasts ranging north and south along the national territory are also directly located on the South China Sea, hit and damaged by typhoons a lot of times during August to October.

The World Bank (2010) pointed out that as a socio-economic condition of Vietnam, there is no diversification of income sources among the regions, since the livelihood in most of the 8 regions depend on climate-sensitive resources. In Northeast, Northwest and Central Highlands, people make their livelihood from rainfed agriculture. Aquaculture is also the major living resource in Mekong River Delta, South Central Coast and North Central Coast. Rainfed agriculture and aquaculture are more sensitive to climate changes than another means of subsistence, which directly affects the living standards of the farmers.

3. 2. Seasonality

Climate is subject to seasonality, a historical pattern that is indicated by a constant frequency

Source : https://pixers.dk/fototapeter/
vietnam-kort-56975533
Figure 3 : Regions in Vietnam

of climate phenomenon. When a climate measure deviates from the observed seasonality, the deviation can be detected as the result of a climate change.

We measure average temperature and rainfall for each of three decades: 1901-1930, 1931-1960, 1961-1990 and 1991-2015 (the recent year), using the monthly data from *Climate Change Knowledge Portal,* The World Bank (Figure 4 and Figure 5).

It is evident that the temperature during a recent period after 1991 is on average higher throughout the year than during another period. The difference is comparable to 0.587 degrees in Celsius higher in October than 1931-1960, 0.796℃ higher in February than 1961-1990, and 0.907℃ higher in February than 1901-1930. Compared with *the Stern Review* saying that the earth has already warmed by 0.7 ℃ since around 1900, those figures suggest that warmth in Vietnam has been increasing more rapidly than on the earth since 1990.

As for the average rainfall measure, there look some monthly variations in the seasonal changes. In January, March, July, November and December, the recent period 1990-2015 recorded more rainfall than another periods, pluvial especially in July, November and December. It i s often that the differences amount to higher levels of 30 millimeters compared to another periods.

3. 3. Trends in Temperature and Rainfall

The tangible changes in the climate seasonality indicate possibility of climate changes in Vietnam. We detect below the changes with two statistical methods. One is the Wilcoxon rank-sum (Mann-Whitney) test for differential trends between two samples. The other method is the Sen's slope for changes in a variable over a time period (Taxak et al. 2014).

We look at temperature trend and the turning point in Vietnam during the period 1901-2016 in Figure 6. Casual observations on the time series data make us to split the whole period into two ones before and after a turning point 1971.

We then do a two-sample Wilcoxon rank-sum (Mann-Whitney) test for both split periods. The first time of changing year on a time series of temperature in Vietnam during the former period 1901-1971 turns

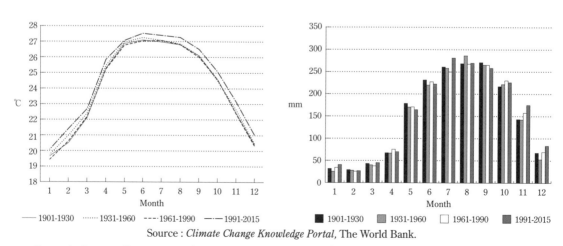

Source : *Climate Change Knowledge Portal,* The World Bank.

Figure 4 : Average Temperatures in Vietnam   Figure 5 : Average Rainfalls in Vietnam out to be 1955 (Figure 7), since a null hypothesis that annual temperature trend of Vietnam of a period 1901-1955 is the same as the trend of the other period 1956-1971 is rejected. The alternative hypothesis is that annual temperature trend of Vietnam of period 1901-1955 is not the same as the trend of period 1956-1971. The estimated test statistics z rejects the null hypothesis, meaning a change in the time series temperature in Vietnam occurred in 1955 (Table 1).

Similarly for the other 1955-2016 sample, the two-sample Wilcoxon rank-sum test results in the second change in the temperature in 1971 (Figure 8). The test statistics z suggests a null hypothesis that annual temperature trend for a period 1955-1971 is the same as the trend of period 1972-2016, against the alternative that the trend for a period 1955-1971 is not the same as for a period 1972-2016 (Table 2).

We detected twice of the turning point in the average temperature for a whole period 1901-2016.

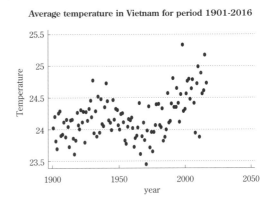

Figure 6 : Average Temperature in Vietnam for a period 1901-2016

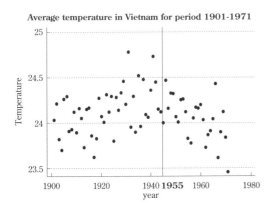

Figure 7 : First Turning Year of Average Temperature in Vietnam: 1955

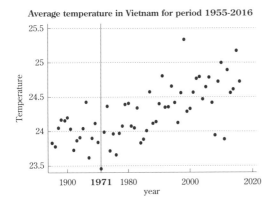

Figure 8 : Second Turning Year of Average Temperature in Vietnam: 1971

Table 1 : Two-Sample Wilcoxon Rank-Sum (Mann-Whitney) Test for 1901-1971

temp_viet_~d	obs	rank sum	expected
1	55	2,154	1,980
2	16	402	576
combined	71	2,556	2,556

unadjusted variance	5,280.00
adjustment for ties	−4.16
adjusted variance	5,275.84

$z = 2.396$
$\text{Prob} > |z| = 0.0166$

Table 2 : Two-Sample Wilcoxon Rank-Sum (Mann-Whitney) Test for 1955-2016

temp_viet_~d	obs	rank sum	expected
1	17	294.5	535.5
2	45	1,658.5	1,417.5
combined	62	1,953	1,953

unadjusted variance	4,016.25
adjustment for ties	−1.11
adjusted variance	4,015.14

$z = -3.803$
$\text{Prob} > |z| = 0.0001$

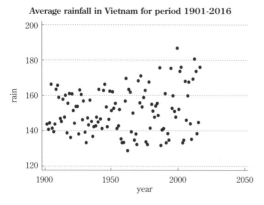

rain_viet_~d	obs	rank sum	expected
1	62	3,416	3,627
2	54	3,370	3,159
combined	116	6,786	6,786

unadjusted variance   32,643.00
adjustment for ties   −0.13
adjusted variance   32,642.87

$z = -1.168$
$\text{Prob} > |z| = 0.2429$

Table 3 : Two-Sample Wilcoxon Rank-Sum (Mann-Whitney) Test for 1901-2016

Figure 9 : Average Rainfall in Vietnam for a period 1901-2016

The same test for the average rainfall in Vietnam, however, cannot detect any probable change years. With the distribution of the average rainfall during the period of 1901-2016 in Figure 9, suppose that there exist the turning point on rainfall in Vietnam in 1962. Then the test statistics suggests a rejection of a null hypothesis annual rainfall trend for a period 1901-1962 is the same as the trend of period 1963-2016 (Table 3). The result shows that the annual rainfall in Vietnam does not have any turning point.

3. 4. Changes in Regional Climate

Next we apply the Sen's slope to the regional data on temperature and rainfall for three sub-periods: 2005-2010, 2005-2014 and 2005-2016. The Sen's slope estimator (Sen 1968) is calculated as the median of the N values of

$$Q_i = \frac{(x_j - x_k)}{(j-k)} \text{ for } i = 1, \cdots, N$$

where x_j, x_k are data values at times j and k ($<j$) for the number of time periods n[2]. In the case of Vietnam, we consider 3 sub-periods which are 2005-2010; 2005-2014; and 2005-2016. Our reference year to consider the climate changes is set to 2005.

Table 4 presents a summary of the estimation results of the Sen's slope of temperature and rainfall of the whole country a nd by 6 regions.

As you can see, there are some climate anomalies at some regions as well as in the whole country. Regardless of the sub-periods, the rainfall has upward time-trends during winter season in nation-wide scale. Regarding the temperature, during fall or winter season the nation records upward time-trends.

Considering the geographical characteristics in Vietnam, we find some contrary climate changes in the regions depending on climate-sensitive resources. In the Central Coast regions with dependency of rainfed agriculture, the rainfall during summer or fall has been scarce and the temperature has been

---

[2] Using the Sen's slope to measuring the change over time is a common ways for many research. The Sen's slope enables us to know changes of a variable over a period of time, particularly for the research in the areas of climate and environment.

Chapter 3   Climate Changes and the Living Standards: A Regional-Scale Assessment of the Vulnerability in Vietnam   43

Table 4 : Sen's Slope of Temperature and Rainfall by 6 Regions for 3 Sub-Periods: 2005-2010; 2005-2014; 2005-2016

By region	Temperature (℃)					Rainfall (mm)				
	Annual	Spring	Summer	Fall	Winter	Annual	Spring	Summer	Fall	Winter
Period 2005-2010										
Whole country	**0.09**	**−0.03**	**0.23**	**0.32**	**−0.06**	**−0.01**	**0.07**	**0.03**	**−0.07**	**0.84**
Red river	0.01	0.01	0.38	0.38	−0.11	−0.05	0.05	0.03	−0.14	0.60
North midland	0.10	−0.09	0.25	0.31	−0.15	−0.08	0.03	0.07	−0.16	0.75
Central coast	0.07	0.08	0.14	0.40	−0.09	0.11	0.05	0.31	0.02	0.84
Central highland	0.39	−0.36	0.09	0.28	−0.03	−0.19	0.21	−0.15	−0.29	1.07
Southeast	0.24	0.16	0.09	0.16	−0.19	0.18	0.28	−0.31	0.36	0.90
Mekong river	−0.02	−0.09	0.29	0.27	0.14	−0.08	−0.01	−0.08	−0.10	1.03
Period 2005-2014										
Whole country	**0.04**	**0.02**	**0.12**	**0.09**	**0.16**	**0.01**	**0.09**	**0.09**	**−0.06**	**0.49**
Red river	0.11	0.26	0.01	0.09	0.10	0.23	0.27	0.20	0.15	0.45
North midland	0.13	0.12	0.01	0.08	0.07	0.10	−0.03	0.11	0.11	0.49
Central coast	−0.12	−0.05	0.06	0.07	0.12	−0.09	−0.08	0.17	−0.17	0.45
Central highland	0.14	−0.08	0.20	0.16	0.21	0.02	0.23	0.22	−0.23	0.56
Southeast	0.13	0.23	0.23	0.10	0.13	0.23	0.25	0.05	0.09	0.63
Mekong river	−0.03	−0.29	0.33	0.11	0.35	−0.29	0.15	−0.16	−0.32	0.49
Period 2005-2016										
Whole country	**0.11**	**−0.02**	**0.33**	**0.06**	**0.34**	**0.02**	**0.00**	**0.00**	**−0.03**	**0.60**
Red river	0.26	0.26	0.26	0.05	0.32	0.28	0.28	0.13	0.21	0.64
North midland	0.27	−0.02	0.26	0.05	0.31	0.07	−0.02	−0.04	0.07	0.60
Central coast	0.09	−0.15	0.25	−0.02	0.24	−0.08	−0.08	0.03	−0.19	0.63
Central highland	0.01	−0.15	0.38	0.20	0.37	−0.09	0.00	0.19	−0.23	0.58
Southeast	0.05	0.24	0.45	0.13	0.34	0.20	−0.07	−0.01	0.23	0.68
Mekong river	−0.10	−0.20	0.49	0.09	0.49	−0.21	−0.11	−0.15	−0.22	0.48

lower in spring season. The similar unfavorable climates have also cast negative impacts on the Mekong River Delta with the primary livelihood of aquaculture and rice-production. In the Red River area with the fertile rice-producing farmers, the temperature shows anomalous warmth for spring to fall seasons. The exposures of the regional-scale climate stress may affect the potential impacts in Vietnam.

4. Close Look at the Living Standards of the Vietnamese Households

In order to estimate the economic effects of the climate changes in Vietnam, we take a close look at the proxies for the living standards. We choose the household incomes by sources and the consumption expenditures, using the dataset of Vietnamese Household Living Standard Survey (VHLSS)[3]. The sample size and the panel sample rate are tabulated in Table 5.

The VHLSS data covers a number of provinces in the whole country and a number of districts and communes by province (Table 6 on the number of administrative units as of December 31, 2016 by province). It

---

3   A recent users' manual of Vietnamese Household Living Standard Survey (VHLSS) is downloadable at http://www. sinfonica.or.jp/information/research/vietnam/Manual_VHLSS_overall_v1.1.pdf

Table 5 : VHLSS Data, General Statistics Office of Vietnam

Year	1992	1998	2002	2004	2006	2008	2010	2012	2014	2016
Sample size (*Households*)	4,799	5,999	29,530	9,188	9,189	9,189	9,399	9,399	9,399	9,399
Panel sample size (*Households*)	no panel	no panel	no panel	4,476	4,298	4,104	no panel	4,173	4,217	4,292
Panel rate (%)				48.7	46.8	44.7		44.4	44.9	45.7

Table 6 : Number of Administrative Units as of 31 December 2016 by Province, VHLSS

		Number of provinces/cities	Number of districts by province	Number of communes by province
Whole Country		**63**	**713**	**11,162**
Region I	Red River Delta	11	130	2,458
Region II	Northern midlands and mountain areas	14	141	2,566
Region III	North central and Central coastal areas	14	174	2,916
Region IV	Central Highlands	5	62	726
Region V	South East	6	72	872
Region VI	Mekong River Delta	13	134	1,624

provides detailed income sources from wage, agriculture land for rent, agriculture activities, forestry activities, fishery activities, non-agriculture activities, and other sources.

The data also contains information on the household expenditures for each categorized consumption: food; garments, clothing and footwear; housing construction material; housing equipment and durables; health service and medicine; education; and other items.

4. 1. Household Incomes by Sources

Table 7 tabulates household incomes by sources within 12 months each year. We pick up three recent years, 2010, 2014 and 2016. The nation-wide average figures indicate the income shares during the period are over a half for sources from wage and slightly more than a quarter for ones from non-agriculture activities. Among the climate-sensitive activities, the real incomes from agriculture and fishery are shown to moderately increase in 2016 as compared to 2010.

When we divide the country into urban and rural areas, we find some spatially disaggregated changes in the income sources in Table 8. Throughout the sample period, the income shares of the climate-sensitive activities in agriculture, forestry and fishery are higher in the rural area than those in the urban area. While the real incomes from the three climate-sensitive sectors increased in the rural area especially at fishery sector, the real incomes from the urban forestry and fishery activities dropped heavily.

More disaggregated in terms of the territorial divisions, Table 9 indicates the same figures as the previous tables for the six regions. The regional income shares denote similarities to the national averages, in the Red River Delta, North Midland, and Central Coast areas. In another area else than the northern areas above, there are differential income shares, which are highly concentrated on non-agri-

Chapter 3   Climate Changes and the Living Standards: A Regional-Scale Assessment of the Vulnerability in Vietnam   45

Table 7 : Household Income within 12 Months by Sources

Income by sources	Income			Income share			Income increase in 2016 as compared to 2010 (excluding CPI increase)
	2010	2014	2016	2010	2014	2016	
	Million Dongs per year			%			%
Income from wage	26.94	49.85	64.10	50.46	54.22	54.77	89.5
Income from agriculture land for rent	0.19	0.31	0.36	0.35	0.34	0.31	43.5
Income from agriculture activities	0.01	0.02	0.02	0.03	0.02	0.02	14.0
Income from forestry activities	0.65	0.93	0.96	1.21	1.01	0.82	−0.3
Income from fishery activities	1.88	2.90	3.43	3.53	3.15	2.93	33.6
Income from non-agriculture activities	14.56	25.07	31.52	27.27	27.27	26.93	68.0
Income from other sources	9.16	12.86	16.65	17.16	13.98	14.23	33.3
Total household income	**53.39**	**91.93**	**117.03**	100.00	100.00	100.00	**70.8**

Table 8 : Household Income within 12 Months in Urban and Rural Areas by Sources

Income by sources	Income			Income share			Income increase in 2016 as compared to 2010 (excluding CPI increase)
	2010	2014	2016	2010	2014	2016	
	Million Dongs per year			%			%
In urban area							
Income from wage	51.22	85.87	111.25	54.03	57.35	57.35	68.7
Income from agriculture land for rent	0.16	0.23	0.27	0.17	0.15	0.14	22.5
Income from agriculture activities	0.005	0.008	0.009	0.01	0.01	0.00	29.6
Income from forestry activities	0.16	0.18	0.12	0.17	0.12	0.06	−75.1
Income from fishery activities	1.01	1.37	1.32	1.07	0.91	0.68	−18.4
Income from non-agriculture activities	26.84	43.75	56.11	28.31	29.22	28.92	60.6
Income from other sources	15.40	18.33	24.92	16.24	12.24	12.84	13.3
Total household income	**94.80**	**149.73**	**193.99**	100.00	100.00	100.00	**56.2**
In rural area							
Income from wage	17.61	34.98	43.59	46.99	51.39	52.17	99.1
Income from agriculture land for rent	0.20	0.35	0.40	0.53	0.51	0.47	52.2
Income from agriculture activities	0.02	0.02	0.03	0.05	0.04	0.03	16.2
Income from forestry activities	0.83	1.24	1.32	2.22	1.82	1.58	10.5
Income from fishery activities	2.22	3.53	4.35	5.92	5.19	5.20	47.5
Income from non-agriculture activities	9.84	17.35	20.83	26.26	25.49	24.92	63.1
Income from other sources	6.76	10.59	13.06	18.04	15.56	15.62	44.6
Total household income	**37.48**	**68.07**	**83.57**	100.00	100.00	100.00	**74.5**

culture (Central Highland), more dependent (Southeast) and less (Mekong River Delta) of the wage incomes.

We can pin down the regional relative changes in the real incomes from the climate-sensitive activities including agriculture land for rent. The stagnant urban activities are noticeable at forestry sectors in the Red River Delta, Central Highland, Southeast and the Mekong River Delta, and at fishery sectors in Central Coast and Central Highland. Among the stagnant cases, Central Highland and the Mekong River Delta suffer from the exposures of lower temperature and less rainfall. The forestry and fishery

Table 9 : Household Income within 12 Months in 6 Regions by Sources

Income by sources	Income			Income share			Income increase in 2016 as compared to 2010 (excluding CPI increase)
	2010	2014	2016	2010	2014	2016	
	Million Dongs per year			%			%
Red River Delta							
Income from wage	36.41	64.00	87.10	54.91	56.20	56.75	90.76
Income from agriculture land for rent	0.095	0.097	0.097	0.14	0.09	0.06	−46.48
Income from agriculture activities	0.009	0.014	0.015	0.01	0.01	0.01	22.34
Income from forestry activities	0.059	0.065	0.058	0.09	0.06	0.04	−50.76
Income from fishery activities	0.68	1.92	2.84	1.03	1.69	1.85	269.71
Income from non-agriculture activities	18.56	30.44	41.24	27.99	26.73	26.87	73.73
Income from other sources	10.50	17.35	22.12	15.83	15.23	14.41	62.27
Total household income	**66.31**	**113.89**	**153.47**	100.00	100.00	100.00	**82.99**
North midland							
Income from wage	17.94	36.48	44.95	56.09	58.15	58.14	102.12
Income from agriculture land for rent	0.05	0.06	0.05	0.16	0.10	0.07	−40.66
Income from agriculture activities	0.01	0.02	0.02	0.04	0.03	0.03	16.77
Income from forestry activities	2.07	3.06	3.42	6.46	4.88	4.42	16.80
Income from fishery activities	0.51	0.82	1.31	1.61	1.30	1.69	105.43
Income from non-agriculture activities	6.53	15.69	17.86	20.40	25.01	23.10	125.20
Income from other sources	4.87	6.60	9.71	15.24	10.52	12.56	50.82
Total household income	**31.99**	**62.74**	**77.32**	100.00	100.00	100.00	**93.29**
Central Coast							
Income from wage	23.38	46.68	56.38	50.20	54.86	54.97	92.73
Income from agriculture land for rent	0.057	0.100	0.150	0.12	0.12	0.15	113.96
Income from agriculture activities	0.010	0.015	0.016	0.02	0.02	0.02	15.14
Income from forestry activities	0.79	1.23	1.13	1.70	1.45	1.10	−5.94
Income from fishery activities	1.96	2.80	2.53	4.21	3.29	2.47	−19.35
Income from non-agriculture activities	12.62	21.89	27.33	27.10	25.73	26.65	68.15
Income from other sources	7.75	12.36	15.04	16.64	14.53	14.66	45.56
Total household income	**46.56**	**85.08**	**102.57**	100.00	100.00	100.00	**71.84**
Central Highland							
Income from wage	18.52	34.15	44.64	52.99	54.91	57.22	92.65
Income from agriculture land for rent	0.244	0.158	0.126	0.70	0.25	0.16	−96.79
Income from agriculture activities	0.023	0.044	0.047	0.07	0.07	0.06	51.50
Income from forestry activities	0.57	0.76	0.61	1.63	1.22	0.78	−42.21
Income from fishery activities	0.48	0.27	0.29	1.39	0.43	0.37	−89.08
Income from non-agriculture activities	11.45	20.67	25.53	32.77	33.24	32.72	74.51
Income from other sources	3.66	6.14	6.78	10.46	9.88	8.69	37.00
Total household income	**34.95**	**62.19**	**78.02**	100.00	100.00	100.00	**74.81**
Southeast							
Income from wage	48.92	84.41	110.22	52.22	60.53	59.70	76.84
Income from agriculture land for rent	0.145	0.267	0.301	0.15	0.19	0.16	59.08
Income from agriculture activities	0.021	0.019	0.022	0.02	0.01	0.01	−45.83
Income from forestry activities	0.06	0.11	0.08	0.07	0.08	0.05	−16.49
Income from fishery activities	0.60	0.71	0.80	0.64	0.51	0.43	−15.15
Income from non-agriculture activities	25.58	39.01	50.76	27.31	27.97	27.49	49.94
Income from other sources	18.35	14.93	22.43	19.59	10.70	12.15	−26.23
Total household income	**93.69**	**139.46**	**184.61**	100.00	100.00	100.00	**48.60**
Mekong River Delta							
Income from wage	19.82	35.82	44.45	39.01	41.99	43.10	75.80
Income from agriculture land for rent	0.55	1.09	1.28	1.08	1.28	1.24	83.86
Income from agriculture activities	0.015	0.024	0.028	0.03	0.03	0.03	35.01
Income from forestry activities	0.182	0.139	0.163	0.36	0.16	0.16	−58.94
Income from fishery activities	5.49	8.10	9.71	10.81	9.50	9.41	28.30
Income from non-agriculture activities	14.70	24.85	28.70	28.94	29.14	27.83	46.79
Income from other sources	10.04	15.27	18.81	19.77	17.90	18.24	38.84
Total household income	**50.81**	**85.30**	103.14	100.00	100.00	100.00	**54.56**

Chapter 3   Climate Changes and the Living Standards: A Regional-Scale Assessment of the Vulnerability in Vietnam   47

sectors in the two areas might be sensitive to the climate exposures, which involves the potential impacts of the climate changes.

It is also noted that the active activities in the rural fishery sectors are in the Red River Delta and North Midland. In these two regions, there are also land use changes from agriculture for rent, the agriculture land which was translated into Central Coast. The similar land use changes to the northern area are identified in the translation from Central Highland to Southeast and the Mekong River Delta in the southern area, too. The changes in land use in the Red River Delta and Central Highland may result potentially from the sensitivity to the exposures.

4. 2. Household Expenditures by Items

Finally, we describe the household expenditures by items in the same order as the incomes by sources: the national averages; the rural-urban patterns; and the regional similarities/dissimilarities.

Table 10 captures the national averages on the household expenditures by items. The expenditure share is almost near a half for food, around 5% and increasing for housing, construction materials, and slightly less than 10% and decreasing for housing equipment and durables.

We see some rural-urban patterns on the expenditure shares in Table 11 Compared with the rural area, the urban expenditure shares are lower in food or education, and higher in housing, construction materials, or housing equipment and durables. It is distinctive that while in the urban area, the real expenditures on housing equipment and durables are contracting, the real expenditure on education is expanding in the rural area.

The national average shares of expenditures by items are congruent to those in the Red River Delta (Table 12). Among the expenditures, items with the least regional deviations from the national averages are food, and garments, clothing and footwear. Regarding another items, there are some regional

Table 10 : Household Expenditures within 12 Months by Sources

Expenditures	Expenditures			Expenditure shares			Expenditure increase in 2016 as compared to 2010 (excluding CPI increase)
	2010	2014	2016	2010	2014	2016	
	Million Dongs per year			%			%
Food expenditures	27.53	41.49	45.69	48.63	47.82	47.07	17.49
Garments, clothing and footwear expenditures	2.03	3.21	3.64	3.59	3.70	3.75	30.83
Housing, construction materials expenditures	2.04	4.93	6.85	3.60	5.68	7.06	187.92
Housing equipment and durables expenditures	5.65	7.71	8.12	9.97	8.89	8.37	−4.61
Health service and medicine expenditures	2.93	4.24	4.84	5.18	4.89	4.99	16.59
Education expenditures	2.94	4.36	5.06	5.20	5.02	5.22	23.71
Other items expenditures	13.49	20.83	22.85	23.83	24.00	23.54	20.91
Total household expenditures	**56.61**	**86.77**	**97.05**	100.00	100.00	100.00	**22.99**

Table 11 : Household Expenditures within 12 Months in Urban and Rural Areas by Sources

Expenditures	Expenditures			Expenditure shares			Expenditure increase in 2016 as compared to 2010 (excluding CPI increase)
	2010	2014	2016	2010	2014	2016	
	Million Dongs per year			%			%
Urban							
Food expenditures	37.54	55.57	61.37	45.54	46.38	45.43	15.03
Garments, clothing and footwear expenditures	3.00	4.43	5.17	3.64	3.70	3.83	24.00
Housing, construction materials expenditures	3.84	8.19	10.74	4.66	6.84	7.95	131.28
Housing equipment and durables expenditures	8.69	10.55	11.18	10.54	8.80	8.27	−19.80
Health service and medicine expenditures	4.96	6.62	8.04	6.02	5.52	5.95	13.58
Education expenditures	3.69	5.24	6.03	4.48	4.38	4.46	14.90
Other items expenditures	20.72	29.22	32.55	25.13	24.38	24.10	8.64
Total household expenditures	**82.45**	**119.83**	**135.09**	100.00	100.00	100.00	**15.40**
Rural							
Food expenditures	23.69	35.68	38.86	50.74	48.79	48.27	15.63
Garments, clothing and footwear expenditures	1.66	2.71	2.97	3.55	3.71	3.69	30.89
Housing, construction materials expenditures	1.34	3.58	5.16	2.88	4.89	6.41	235.43
Housing equipment and durables expenditures	4.48	6.54	6.79	9.59	8.94	8.43	3.27
Health service and medicine expenditures	2.15	3.26	3.45	4.61	4.46	4.29	11.74
Education expenditures	2.65	3.99	4.64	5.68	5.46	5.77	26.57
Other items expenditures	10.71	17.36	18.63	22.95	23.75	23.14	25.44
Total household expenditures	**46.69**	**73.12**	**80.51**	100.00	100.00	100.00	**24.01**

variations in propensities for expenditures. For the expenditures on housing, construction materials, Southeast region is more expansionary than the average, as opposed to being more austere in Central Highland and the Mekong River Delta regions. As for housing equipment and durables, there is a contrast between more expansionary North Midland and more austere Southeast.

The health service and medicine is an item with the widest regional disparities between the more expansionary Central East and Southeast, and the more austere North Midland and the Mekong River Delta. People in North Midland expend less for education than the average, while the Mekong River Delta pays more for education.

The real expenditures on housing, construction materials, on one hand, has surged in the exposed areas, which may be a symptom of adaptive capacity against the climate changes. On the other hand, the negative impacts on housing equipment and durables under the climate exposures might show the vulnerability to the climate changes.

Chapter 3 Climate Changes and the Living Standards: A Regional-Scale Assessment of the Vulnerability in Vietnam   49

Table 12 : Household Expenditures within 12 Months in 6 Regions by Sources

Expenditures	Expenditures			Expenditure shares			Expenditure increase in 2016 as compared to 2010 (excluding CPI increase)
	2010	2014	2016	2010	2014	2016	
	Million Dongs per year			%			%
Red River Delta							
Food expenditures	30.97	46.29	48.92	47.19	46.73	45.04	9.49
Garments, clothing and footwear expenditures	2.47	4.00	4.21	3.76	4.04	3.88	22.19
Housing, construction materials expenditures	2.34	6.57	8.83	3.57	6.63	8.13	228.86
Housing equipment and durables expenditures	7.33	8.12	9.18	11.16	8.20	8.45	−23.18
Health service and medicine expenditures	3.64	5.63	6.50	5.55	5.68	5.99	30.07
Education expenditures	3.44	5.19	6.52	5.23	5.24	6.00	41.33
Other items expenditures	15.45	23.26	24.45	23.54	23.48	22.51	9.82
Total household expenditures	**65.64**	**99.06**	**108.62**	**100.00**	**100.00**	**100.00**	**17.03**
North midland							
Food expenditures	23.47	35.97	40.42	52.87	47.43	47.83	23.74
Garments, clothing and footwear expenditures	1.83	3.04	3.46	4.13	4.01	4.09	40.29
Housing, construction materials expenditures	1.24	3.44	6.96	2.80	4.54	8.24	411.25
Housing equipment and durables expenditures	4.69	11.36	9.42	10.57	14.98	11.15	52.28
Health service and medicine expenditures	1.66	2.63	2.82	3.73	3.46	3.34	21.86
Education expenditures	1.79	3.29	3.36	4.04	4.33	3.97	38.93
Other items expenditures	9.71	16.12	18.07	21.86	21.26	21.38	37.72
Total household expenditures	**44.40**	**75.85**	**84.51**	**100.00**	**100.00**	**100.00**	**41.90**
Central Coast							
Food expenditures	26.41	41.58	44.57	49.65	50.10	49.61	20.30
Garments, clothing and footwear expenditures	1.79	2.97	3.38	3.37	3.58	3.76	40.09
Housing, construction materials expenditures	1.55	4.26	5.92	2.92	5.13	6.59	233.46
Housing equipment and durables expenditures	5.78	6.32	6.73	10.86	7.61	7.49	−31.93
Health service and medicine expenditures	3.17	4.65	4.74	5.95	5.60	5.28	1.32
Education expenditures	2.83	4.38	4.61	5.33	5.27	5.14	14.38
Other items expenditures	11.66	18.85	19.88	21.93	22.71	22.13	22.01
Total household expenditures	**53.19**	**83.00**	**89.84**	**100.00**	**100.00**	**100.00**	**20.44**
Central Highland							
Food expenditures	27.39	39.08	42.22	50.79	45.23	47.65	5.69
Garments, clothing and footwear expenditures	2.21	3.30	3.74	4.11	3.82	4.23	20.65
Housing, construction materials expenditures	1.38	4.58	3.83	2.56	5.30	4.33	129.73
Housing equipment and durables expenditures	4.28	9.17	5.66	7.94	10.61	6.39	−16.19
Health service and medicine expenditures	3.21	5.43	5.22	5.95	6.28	5.90	14.31
Education expenditures	2.88	4.17	4.80	5.34	4.82	5.42	18.24
Other items expenditures	12.58	20.69	23.11	23.32	23.94	26.09	35.30
Total household expenditures	**53.93**	**86.41**	**88.59**	**100.00**	**100.00**	**100.00**	**15.83**
Southeast							
Food expenditures	32.84	49.90	59.56	44.00	46.63	46.32	32.90
Garments, clothing and footwear expenditures	2.43	3.37	4.34	3.25	3.15	3.37	30.38
Housing, construction materials expenditures	4.48	7.07	9.24	6.01	6.61	7.19	57.65
Housing equipment and durables expenditures	5.80	8.14	9.56	7.76	7.60	7.43	16.43
Health service and medicine expenditures	5.16	5.48	7.72	6.91	5.12	6.00	1.19
Education expenditures	4.04	4.30	5.31	5.42	4.02	4.13	−17.13
Other items expenditures	19.90	28.75	32.87	26.66	26.87	25.56	16.70
Total household expenditures	**74.65**	**107.01**	**128.59**	**100.00**	**100.00**	**100.00**	**23.81**
Mekong River Delta							
Food expenditures	25.89	37.15	41.20	49.03	48.83	46.66	10.66
Garments, clothing and footwear expenditures	1.73	2.66	3.03	3.27	3.50	3.43	26.64
Housing, construction materials expenditures	1.86	4.14	5.28	3.52	5.44	5.98	135.59
Housing equipment and durables expenditures	4.96	4.82	7.39	9.39	6.33	8.37	0.62
Health service and medicine expenditures	1.75	2.61	3.10	3.31	3.43	3.51	29.34
Education expenditures	2.98	4.49	5.46	5.65	5.90	6.19	34.70
Other items expenditures	13.64	20.21	22.83	25.84	26.57	25.86	18.92
Total household expenditures	**52.81**	**76.08**	**88.29**	**100.00**	**100.00**	**100.00**	**18.75**

5. Conclusion

We make qualitative conclusions on regional-scale assessment of the vulnerability in Vietnam. It is crucial to distinguish inter-related concepts in the climate change literature. Vulnerability to climate changes is a multidimensional continuum characterized by a function of exposure, sensitivity and adaptability. Our assessment suggests that the exposures some regions face in Vietnam are lower temperature or less precipitation. The forestry and fishery sectors in the Central Highland and the Mekong River Delta are sensitive to the climate changes. The exposure in the Red River and Central Highland may also change the land use from agriculture for rent.

An expenditure surge in the housing, construction materials might be a symptom of adaptive capacity, while the negative impacts on housing equipment and durables in the Red River Delta, Central Coast and Central Highland are possibly the vulnerability in the Vietnam.

Based on the assessment, we wonder what heterogeneous attributes on households are sensitive to climate vulnerability. Our candidates are family size, family composition, labor market status, occupation, education or so. We will proceed in the next paper to an empirical analysis on household-level Engel curves (Deaton and Muellbauer 1980; Blundell et al. 1993; Banks et al 1997; Blundell et al. 2007) to identify household attributes vulnerable to the climate changes.

References

Banks, J., R. Blundell, and A. Lewbel (1997), "Quadratic Engel Curves and Consumer Demand," *The Review of Economics and Statistics,* 79(4), pp.527-539.

Blundell, R., P. Pashardes, and G. Weber (1993), "What Do We Learn about Consumer Demand Patterns from Micro Data?" *The American Economic Review,* 83(3), pp.570-597.

Blundell, R., and T. Stoker (2007), "Models of Aggregate Economic Relationships that Account for Heterogeneity," Chapter 68 in *Handbook of Econometrics,* vol.6A, pp.4609-4666.

Deaton, A., and J. Muellbauer (1980), "An Almost Ideal Demand System," *The American Economic Review,* 70(3), pp.312-326.

Fritzsche, K., S. Schneiderbauer, P. Buseck, S. Kienberger, M. Buth, M. Zebisch, and W. Kahlenborn (2014), *The Vulnerability Sourcebook,* Deutsche Gesellschaft für Internationale Zusammenarbeit (GIZ) GmbH.

Gibson, C. C., E. Ostrom, and T. K. Ahn (2000), "The Concept of Scale and the Human Dimensions of Global Change: A Survey," *Ecological Economics,* 32, pp.217-239.

Mani, M., S. Bandyopadhyay, S. Chonabayashi, A. Markandya, and T. Mosier (2018), *South Asia's Hotspots: The Impact of Temperature and Precipitation Changes on Living Standards,* Washington, DC: The World Bank.

O'Brien, K., L. Sygna, and J. E. Haugen (2004), "Vulnerable or Resilient? A Multi-Scale Assessment of Climate Impacts and Vulnerability in Norway," *Climate Change,* 64, pp.193-225.

Sen, P. K. (1968), "Estimates of the Regression Coefficient Based on Kendall's Tau," *Journal of the American Statistical Association,* 63, pp.1379-1389.

Stern, N. (2007), *The Economics of Climate Change: The Stern Review,* Cambridge: Cambridge University Press.

Taxak, A. K., A. R. Murumkar, and D. S. Arya (2014), "Long Term Spatial and Temporal Rainfall Trends and

Homogeneity Analysis in Wainganga Basin, Central India," *Weather and Climate Extremes,* 4, pp.50-61.

The World Bank (2010), *Economics of Adaptation to Climate Change, Vietnam,* Washington, DC: The World Bank.

Tol, R. S. J. (2009), "The Economic Effects of Climate Change," *The Journal of Economic Perspectives,* 23(2), pp.29-51.

United Nations Development Programme (2015), *Viet Nam Special Report on Managing the Risks of Extreme Events and Disasters to Advance Climate Change Adaptation*, Viet Nam Publishing House of Natural Resources Environment and Cartography, Ha Noi, Viet Nam.

Chapter 4

Consumption Smoothing in the Aftermath of the 2014 Coup d'état in the Thai Urban and Rural Areas : A Preliminary Estimation[1]

Ichihiro UCHIDA, Yosuke TAKEDA, and Hiroyuki SHIBUSAWA

Abstract

Closely following Kinnan and Townsend (2012), this paper estimates effects of the Thai 2014 coup d'état on the consumption insurance. The estimation with data of the Household Annual Resurvey 2014 and 2015, shows that while the urban households are fully insured, the rural ones are not fully insured against income fluctuations. Co-movements of house repair, education and clothing expenses with the revenue are encountered by the rural households. On the other hand, the households in rural area were to larger extent insured in 2015 after the Thai 2014 coup. A role of the financial networks in consumption smoothing were less effective in the rural area. These drastic changes may be attributed to a policy change in the rice pledge loan scheme, the repayments for the loans which had been deterred before the 2014 coup and was met after the coup.

JEL : R11, R20, Q12, Q14, D12

Keywords : Kinship Network, Financial Access, Consumption Smoothing

1. Introduction

We estimate a standard equation for consumption smoothing against income fluctuations specified and applied to the 1999-2005 Thai villages by Kinnan and Townsend (2012). Their estimation using the sample for 1999-2005 monthly data showed how large reductions in consumption-income co-movement are yielded by accesses to financial networks. Financial networks, especially ones based on kinships are risk-sharing schemes for the villagers who are exposed to income risks without formal finances.

We pay special attention in this paper to the effects of the coup d'état in 2014, Thailand. The recent Thai coup occurred in the multiparty democratic polity. This paper explore what effects a change in political institutions after the coup had on the consumption smoothing via financial networks? Are there any regional differences in the economic consequences of the political change? In order to consider these questions, we follow the previous paper Kinnan and Townsend (2012) as dutifully as possible. The exceptions are for estimation sample-period and some significant changes leading to our own contributions, as described below.

---

1 We are grateful for inspiring comments to Rikiya Matsukura, Nihon University the discussant in the Center for China and Asian Studies International Workshop on "Japanese Companies Operating and Local Consumer Behavior in East Asia" on 9-10th of December 2017, Hanoi, Vietnam, especially to the discussant Rikiya Matsukura, Nihon University. We also thank Dr. Sombat Sakunthasathien, Director of the Thai Family Research Project and his colleagues for welcoming our visit of their sites in LopBuri and Chacheongsao provinces for the survey at the Townsend Thai Project, from 5th to 6th July 2016. Their generosity in letting us observe the enumerators' contact with respondents to the detailed survey, could extract useful information for this research.

Why are we interested in the 2014 coup? In view of the chronic political turmoil in Thai, the country during the sample period 1999-2005 remained still in a multiparty democracy. When a major financial crisis hit the one of the High-Performing Asia Economies in 1997, the currency baht was devalued and despite the IMF's rescue program, the economy had deteriorated which bankruptcy and unemployment followed by 1998, partly because of the government austere fiscal policy. During the financial turmoil, however, the transfer of political power had been in a democratic process without military interventions. In particular, since the first-ever elections to the Senate were held in 2000, the *Thai Rak Thai* party had dominated the political majority under a leadership of Thaksin Shinawatra in exchange for his populist social programs. Thaksin continued as the Prime Minister up to 2006, when the military set up a successful coup on the background of mass protests over his corruption issues.

In sharp contrast to the relatively calm period 1999-2005 in Thai that Kinnan and Townsend (2012) turned into their empirical analysis, the year 2014 is a critical moment when political instability brought about the military coup d'état on May 22. The coup was launched by General Prayut Chan-o-cha who as head got the National Council for Peace and Order (NCPO) establish a military-dominated national legislature. Prior to the 2014 coup for the caretaker Prime Minister Yingluck Shinawatra, the rice-pledge scheme had been a significant budgetary problem that the government pledged to support rice farmers with a plan to purchase rice at above market prices, but could not afford to pay rice farmers seeking deferred compensation from the Bank for Agriculture and Agricultural Co-operatives (BAAC). The NCPO leader Prayut then announced to dismiss all the rice price-support schemes, followed by payments for all the arrears of 92.4 billion baht starting in May, 2014.

It should be considered to be a social experiment that in the aftermath of the 2104 coup, there was a drastic change in the distributive scheme for the Thai rice farmers. They are ordinarily thought to live in some rural area where the agriculture farms are run partly via informal lending or borrowing of free labor, equipment or money between altruistic extended family members. Our research thus aims at probable changes in a role of informal finance in consumption smoothing in the Thai post-2014 coup period.

We draw on the Townsend Thai Project, which is currently continuing and zealously collecting rich data on the Thai villagers to bridge the divide between policy and research (Townsend et al. 2013; Townsend 2016). The data provides us an opportunity of evidence-based assessment on policy changes in Thailand. Since we are interested in the effects of the 2014 coup on consumption smoothing in Thai, our data choice is the Household Annual Resurvey 2014 and 2015. The surveys are separated into area coverages of the respondents, rural and urban. Therefore, using the Household Annual Resurvey 2014 and 2015 in the Townsend Thai Project Data, we estimate changes in the relationships between consumption smoothing and financial networks in the Thai rural and urban areas, in the aftermath of the 2014 coup d'état.

We make a brief conclusion that the households in rural area were to larger extent insured in 2015 after the Thai 2014 coup. A role of the financial networks in consumption smoothing were less effective in the rural area. These drastic changes may be attributed to a policy change in the rice pledge loan scheme, the repayments for the loans which had been deterred before the 2014 coup and was met after the coup.

The structure of this paper is as follows: in Section 2, we describe detailed differences in estimations from Kinnan and Townsend (2012). Section 3 shows the estimation results. Section 4 concludes this paper.

2. What Differs from Kinnan and Townsend (2012)

Cynthia Kinnan and Robert Townsend, "Kinship and Financial Networks, Formal Financial Access, and Risk Reduction," *American Economic Review: Papers & Proceedings* (2012) is a short paper with less expositions. But it addresses a crucial issue of consumption smoothing in the village economy with formal and informal finances[2]. As well as consumption smoothing to consider, it also investigates the impacts of kinship and formal financial networks on the ability of household as corporate firms to smooth investment in the face of cash flow fluctuations.

The estimated equations for consumption and investment smoothing are ones to allow effects of income fluctuations to depend on the presence of kin and financial networks. The estimation results in demonstrating the co-movements with income smoothing which are reduced by formal financial networks in the case of consumption or kinship-based informal networks in the other case of investment. The asymmetric roles of financial networks in consumption- and investment-smoothing suggest an aspect of 'households as corporate firms.' While the financing needs of consumption can be met effectively by collateralized borrowings that pledges tangible assets, investment-financing is so large that it cannot be collateralized with tangible assets and nonpecuniary punishments by kin are required.

We will describe some detailed differences in data and specification of our estimation from that in Kinnan and Townsend (2012).

2. 1. Data

Kinnan and Townsend (2012) used the household data from the 1999-2005 monthly waves of the Townsend Thai Monthly Survey, covering a total of 531 households in 16 villages. We use annual data of the Household Annual Resurvey 2014 and 2015 (Townsend and Suwanik 2016) conducted in the Townsend Thai Project. It covers 1530 households in urban areas and 1229 ones in rural areas.

Descriptive statistics of the variables we use are shown in 2014 (Table 1 for rural area, and Table 2 for urban

---

2 Among the voluminous related literature, we mention some papers on the issue Kinnan and Townsend (2012) took. Kurosaki and Sawada (1999) demonstrated whether household consumption in rural Pakistan is affected by income fluctuations. First, idiosyncratic shocks occurring inside the rural areas are mutually insured more than expected. Second, risk sharing in agricultural villages in Pakistan does not happen as the area becomes wider. The results indicate that public investment / public intervention, which promotes pooling of risks beyond the village area, is important. Munshi (2011) proposed an informal institutional mechanism -the community-based network-through which families belonging to the same neighborhood or kinship group can bootstrap their way out of such low-skill occupational traps in Indian data. Occupational traps indicate that families in low-skill with low levels of human capital can stay poor one generation to the next, while families in high-skill occupations with correspondingly high levels of human capital stay wealthy, despite being endowed with the same level of ability on average. Chuang and Schechter (2015) also review the empirical literature in developing countries using explicit social network data. They focus on social networks as conduits for both monetary transfers and information.

area) and 2015 (Table 3 for rural area, and Table 4 for urban area). The mean values of total consumption in the course of 2014 are 34 thousand baht for the rural areas and 48 thousand baht for the urban areas. The means of gross revenue in 2014 are also 391 thousand baht for rural and 582 thousand baht for urban areas. In terms of the consumption and revenue, the figures indicate great regional disparities in Thailand.

2. 1. 1. Sample Period

As we mentioned above, the aftermath of the 2104 coup is a social experiment for us to estimate a drastic change in the distributive scheme for the Thai households including rice farmers living in the rural area with informal or formal lending or borrowing. Since probable changes in a role of informal finance in consumption smoothing in the Thai post-2014 coup period is our interest, our sample period should cover periods before and after the 2014 coup.

On the other hand, the sample period 1999-2005 Kinnan and Townsend (2012) covered is the relatively calm period with a multiparty democracy, in view of the chronic political turmoil in Thailand. The sample period is not appropriate for experimenting on the socio-economic changes in such a distributive scheme as the Thai rice pledge loans.

2. 1. 2. Rural vs. Urban Areas

In the Household Annual Resurvey, the surveyed areas is divided into rural areas and urban areas across 6 changwats in 4 regions: Chachoengsao and Lop Buri in the Central region, Buriram and Sisaket in the Northeast region, Satun in the South region, and Phrae in the North region. Figure 1 indicates the spatial arrangement of the surveyed areas.

Note that the distinction between rural and urban areas is based as follows: "in general, urban areas tend to be centers of transportation, i.e., they have more routes directed to and out of more than rural areas have" (Townsend and Suwanik 2016).

As shown in Table 1 and Table 2 above, great regional disparities in Thailand are in the consumption and the revenue. Those in the urban area are more financially comfortable enough to consume more than in the rural area. Table 1 and Table 2 also suggest that a gap opposite to the richness lies in the formal

Source : Townsend and Suwanik (2016).
Figure 1 : Survey Areas in the Townsend Thai Project

Table 1 : Summary Statistics: Rural Area, 2014

	count	mean	sd	max	min
Total consumption	1,200	34,759.71	54,315.01	873,500	200
House repair	1,200	10,337.71	46,697.92	800,000	0
Vehicle repair	1,200	2,718.033	6,399.291	100,000	0
Education expense	1,200	8,106.996	12,803.35	140,000	0
Clothing expense	1,200	2,904.238	3,081.736	35,000	0
Eating outside home	1,200	10,692.74	12,631.27	111,000	0
Gross revenue	1,200	391,144.9	655,379	8,611,320	9,400
Live outside the house (child)	1,200	1.929	1.925	12	0
Parents live outside tambon	1,200	0.222	0.416	1	0
Own loan or not	1,200	0.664	0.472	1	0
Total number of household members	1,200	3.707	1.68	13	1

Table 2 : Summary Statistics: Urban Area, 2014

	count	mean	sd	max	min
Total consumption	1,438	48,075.96	93,014.85	2,031,000	0
House repair	1,438	11,007.02	84,114.68	2,000,000	0
Vehicle repair	1,438	3,354.444	5,780.275	54,000	0
Education expense	1,438	12,012.23	25,660.83	720,000	0
Clothing expense	1,438	3,754.513	3,727.768	55,000	0
Eating outside home	1,438	17,947.74	19,448.88	219,000	0
Gross revenue	1,438	582,238.4	788,457	8,161,200	7,200
Live outside the house (child)	1,438	1.346	1.506	11	0
Parents live outside tambon	1,438	0.207	0.405	1	0
Own loan or not	1,438	0.478	0.5	1	0
Total number of household members	1,438	3.784	1.882	16	1

financial opportunities between urban and rural. The number of households who owe money or goods to anyone is greater in rural than in urban area.

2. 1. 3. Types of Consumption Expenditures

In addition to total consumption, we pick up some types of consumption expenditures: house repair, vehicle repair, education expense, clothing expense, eating outside home.

2. 1. 4. Dummy Variables for Financial Networks

Kinnan and Townsend (2012) measured information on financial networks with twofold data: formal financial network and kinship network. The former measure depicts whether each household borrows directly from either commercial banks or the BAAC or indirectly from someone who borrows from the bank. The indirect financial connection is based on information of 'reachability' between each household. The direct and indirect indicators for formal finance are measured with each dummy variable, 0 or 1. The latter kinship network is also measured from information on the location of the parents, siblings, adult children, and parents' siblings of each household head and its spouse. The measure is similarly a dummy variable equal to 1 if having kin in the same village as the head/spouse or to 0 otherwise.

In our paper, a qualitatively different idea from Kinnan and Townsend (2012) is considered on kinship financial networks. It draws on some works by Mark Rosenzweig on risk sharing mechanisms of rural households (Rosenzweig 1988; Rosenzweig and Stark 1989). In an environment characterized by information costs and spatially covariant risks, households take the marriage of daughters to locally distant, dispersed yet kinship-related households as implicit interhousehold contractual arrangements. Based on the theory and evidence, we take two measures as the kinship network. One is from information on whether the children of the head/spouse live outside the house. From a questionnaire "How many children of the head and/or the spouse live outside the house?" the dummy variable is generated equal to 1 if the answer is not 0 or to 0 otherwise. The other kinship measure is a dummy variable equal to 1 if the head responds 'yes' to a question "Are the head or the spouse's mother and/or father alive and living outside of this tambon?" or to 0 otherwise. We use these two kinship-related risk-sharing measures against the spatially idiosyncratic income risks, typical in Thailand.

As for the formal financial access, we take a dummy variable equal to 1 if the household answers 'yes' to a question "Do you or members of your household owe money or goods to anyone?" or 0 otherwise. The question is accompanied with a caveat "For example, to a commercial bank, the BAAC, a PCG, a Rice Bank, the Agricultural Cooperative, a government agency, a moneylender, a friend, a relative or any other individual or institution." We include as formal finance even friends or relatives as well as the financial intermediaries.

Note that those dummy variables are state variables for financial networks linking the Thai households in 2014 and in 2015. Since 'this past year' in the Household Annual Resurvey 2014 means 'June 2012 to May 2013', it is definitely evident that the state variables in 2014 are ones immune to effects of the 2014 coup d'état. Concerning the 2015 state variables, it contains information on changes in the financial networks stemming from the aftermath of the May 2014 coup. The contrasting informational contents of the state variables in 2014 and 2015 reveals effects of the 2014 coup, as estimated below.

2. 2. Specification

We specify an estimated equation for consumption smoothing against income variations in the same way that Kinnan and Townsend (2012) did. The equation is

$$\Delta C_i = \alpha_1 + \alpha_2 \Delta Y_i + \alpha_3 \Delta Y_i \times k_i + \alpha_4 \Delta Y_i \times f_i + \alpha_5 m_i + \eta_i \text{ for a household i}$$

where ΔC_i and ΔY_i are changes in the per capita consumption (total, house repair, vehicle repair, education expense, clothing expense, or eating outside home) and gross revenue, respectively, and k_i and f_i are the dummy variables representing the states of kinship network and financial access, respectively. A control variable m_i, a change in total number of household members is added to the equation, instead of household's average net worth in a case of Kinnan and Townsend (2012).

In the estimated equation, a null hypothesis of full consumption insurance is $\alpha_2 = 0$. When the consumption smoothing is not fully insured, if the kin-based financial network or the formal financial access reduces the risks against income fluctuation, then the coefficients α_3 or α_4 should be significantly negative.

2. 3 Effects of a Change in Political Institutions

Compared with the descriptive statistics both in 2014 (Table 1 for rural area, and Table 2 for urban area) and 2015 (Table 3 for rural area, and Table 4 for urban area), the largest difference lies in a decline in the average gross revenue in the urban area. The massive decrease in the urban households' annual income amounts to 33 thousand baht on average that is around 6% income-cut. We cannot account for any causes of the revenue drain, but the political turmoil then at Bangkok might spread over the surrounding urban area, too.

Owing to the informational contents of the state variables on financial networks, as mentioned above, we can extract effects of the 2014 coup. Concretely, we estimate the same specification of the equation as above, except for the state variables on the financial networks replaced with the 2015 one instead of 2014.

The hypothetical assumption on the financial structure during a period from 2014 to 2015, that is a social experiment, might reveal what had happened to the Thai consumption insurance if the financial structure were the same as in 2015 when the aftermath of the 2014 coup was stabilized partly via the deterred repayments of the rice-pledging loans from government and abolishment of the scheme.

Note that the 2014 coup might have endogenously influence financial networking formed by the Thai

Table 3 : Summary Statistics: Rural Area, 2015

	count	mean	sd	max	min
Total consumption	1,192	35,873.84	50,497.42	742,000	0
House repair	1,192	7,639.933	42,467.99	700,000	0
Vehicle repair	1,192	2,686.846	5,958.33	120,000	0
Education expense	1,192	8,771.429	14,165.57	120,000	0
Clothing expense	1,192	3,290.562	3,882.55	40,000	0
Eating outside home	1,192	13,485.07	13,025.34	98,000	0
Gross revenue	1,192	403,574.9	1,087,805	31,948,880	10,400
Live outside the house (child)	1,192	1.898	1.914	12	0
Parents live outside tambon	1,192	0.175	0.38	1	0
Own loan or not	1,192	0.627	0.484	1	0
Total number of household members	1,192	3.664	1.676	13	1

Table 4 : Summary Statistics: Urban Area, 2015

	count	mean	sd	max	min
Total consumption	1,422	48,495.95	109,557.2	3,014,000	0
House repair	1,422	9,912.447	102,261.2	3,000,000	0
Vehicle repair	1,422	3,441.062	5,459.099	50,000	0
Education expense	1,422	11,716.86	20,402.75	288,000	0
Clothing expense	1,422	3,924.775	4,087.841	50,000	0
Eating outside home	1,422	19,500.81	22,222.25	250,000	0
Gross revenue	1,422	549,207.7	814,289.2	11,213,000	10,000
Live outside the house (child)	1,422	1.305	1.48	10	0
Parents live outside tambon	1,422	0.205	0.404	1	0
Own loan or not	1,422	0.468	0.499	1	0
Total number of household members	1,422	3.721	1.872	15	1

households as well as the households' consumption behaviors, so that our hypothetical experiment could not be exogenous. If the possibility is correct, we should take into account the endogeneity problem in our estimation. It remains one of our further works[3].

3. Estimation Results

The estimation method is ordinary least squares (OLS) and the standard errors are heteroscedasticity-robust. The estimation results with the total consumption as an explained variable is shown in Table 5.

3. 1. Insurance Against Income Fluctuations

The coefficients on the gross revenue term in the total consumption equation are significantly positive only in rural area. It shows that the urban households are fully insured. On the other hand, the rural ones are not fully insured against income fluctuations. But the magnitude of the consumption/income co-movement in the rural areas is slight. With 1 baht income change, a 0.0083 baht consumption change is associated. The coefficient is quite comparable to the estimate 0.0078 of Kinnan and Townsend (2012).

In a full version of the estimated equation, the coefficient on the revenue term in rural case is a little greater, a 0.0155 baht consumption change in response to 1 baht income change. But the estimated value

Table 5 : Estimation Result (OLS: Total, State Variable for Financial Networks: 2014)

VARIABLES	rural area ΔTotal expenditure	urban area ΔTotal expenditure	rural area ΔTotal expenditure	urban area ΔTotal expenditure
ΔGross revenue	0.0155** (0.0066)	0.0986 (0.0845)	0.0083*** (0.0014)	0.0290 (0.0188)
ΔGross revenue × Live outside the house(Child)	−0.0063 (0.0068)	−0.0200 (0.0431)		
ΔGross revenue × Parents live outside tambon	−0.0137** (0.0065)	0.0011 (0.0210)		
ΔGross Revenue × Own Loan or not	0.0059 (0.0049)	−0.0762 (0.0568)		
ΔTotal number of household members	208.4643 (3,028.1927)	20,643.6063 (15,175.0107)	304.6711 (2,989.4163)	21,548.8273 (15,093.4838)
Constant	1,002.2196 (1,796.9063)	4,453.9693 (4,410.3386)	992.2932 (1,788.8598)	2,960.4151 (3,788.4825)
Observations	1,192	1,422	1,192	1,422
R-squared	0.0163	0.0613	0.0127	0.0325

Note 1 : Heteroskedasticity-robust standard errors in parentheses.
　　 2 : *** $p < 0.01$, ** $p < 0.05$, * $p < 0.1$.

3　Another further work of us is to build a theoretical model on economic consequences of the military coup. Concerning the issue, we have some references, for instance Acemoglu and Robinson 2008 and Acemoglu et al. 2010. They consider a model of the elite as a principle and the military as a 'perfect' agent where de jure and de facto political powers are distributed among them.

is ever smaller than the Kinnan and Townsend's 0.1645.

3. 2. Effects of Informal and Formal Finances

The rural households with parents living outside the same tambon as the head are also better insured than the average. The informal kin-based finance plays even though a negligible role of the consumption insurance in the Thai rural area.

3. 3. Differences Between Rural and Urban Areas

Regarding total consumption, we reported a difference in full consumption insurance between rural and urban. While the urban households are fully insured, the rural ones not fully insured against income fluctuations. The same spatial feature can be found in each type of expenditures (Table 6 and Table 7).

Among the five items of consumption, co-movements of house repair, education and clothing expenses with the revenue are encountered by the rural households. In the urban cases, on the other hand, we cannot find any types of expenditures positively co-move with revenue. The rural households are not fully insured against income fluctuations, while the urban households are fully insured in terms of expenditure types, too.

3. 4. Characteristics in Expenditure Types

Among types of the consumption expenditures, the expenditures for house repair, education, and clothing are not fully insured in the rural area. Out of the three items uninsured against the revenue variations, the house repair and the education are better insured than the average through parents living outside or formal borrowing, respectively.

As for the urban area, the households are not fully insured especially for educational expenditure that they consume less when the revenues increase.

The households with parents living outside the tambon are worse insured than the average concerning the expenditures for education and clothing.

3. 5. Effects of the 2014 Coup d'état

From Table 8, Table 9 and Table 10, it is evident that the households in both of urban and rural areas are fully insured in 2015 when influences of the Thai 2014 coup on the nation were stabilized. Looking at the types of consumption expenditures in 2015, we also find full consumption insurance against income variations, except for educational expense in the rural area. The effects of financial networks on consumption smoothing are less effective than in the rural area before the 2014 coup.

The changes before and after the 2014 coup may be attributed to a policy change in the rice pledge loan scheme, the repayments for the loans which had been deterred before the 2014 coup and was met when the NCPO leader Prayut took office after the coup.

Table 6 : Estimation Result (OLS: Expenditure component, State Variables for Financial Networks: 2014, rural area)

VARIABLES	ΔHouse repair	ΔHouse repair	ΔVehicle repair	ΔVehicle repair	Δeducation expense	Δeducation expense	ΔClothing expense	ΔClothing expense	ΔEating outside home	ΔEating outside home
ΔGross revenue	0.0099 (0.0061)	0.0064*** (0.0015)	0.0009 (0.0014)	0.0002 (0.0002)	0.0035*** (0.0012)	0.0012** (0.0005)	−0.0004 (0.0008)	0.0003** (0.0001)	0.0016 (0.0016)	0.0002 (0.0002)
ΔGross revenue × Live outside the house (Child)	−0.0024 (0.0063)		−0.0013 (0.0014)		−0.0019* (0.0011)		0.0008 (0.0008)		−0.0015 (0.0016)	
ΔGross revenue × Parents live outside tambon	−0.0120** (0.0060)		0.0001 (0.0013)		−0.0010 (0.0012)		0.0002 (0.0009)		−0.0010 (0.0017)	
ΔGross Revenue × Own Loan or not	0.0076 (0.0052)		0.0015 (0.0010)		−0.0037** (0.0017)		0.0004 (0.0004)		0.0001 (0.0012)	
ΔTotal number of household members	−2,535.0049 (2,859.8539)	−2,378.0239 (2,824.0603)	−297.2679 (217.9772)	−257.8680 (215.5501)	1,411.4697** (569.9469)	1,303.7723** (567.2578)	764.1946*** (157.8952)	775.8879*** (165.2584)	865.0728 (870.9170)	860.9027 (869.6621)
Constant	−2,878.2103* (1,673.8069)	−2,947.0927* (1,665.7731)	−25.2947 (219.5610)	−47.1545 (221.6544)	645.6900* (336.7578)	727.2214** (339.5894)	422.8364*** (105.9087)	411.4545*** (106.3024)	2,837.1983*** (364.5502)	2,847.8645*** (365.8482)
Observations	1,192	1,192	1,192	1,192	1,192	1,192	1,192	1,192	1,192	1,192
R-squared	0.0142	0.0093	0.0089	0.0008	0.0245	0.0128	0.0320	0.0267	0.0030	0.0023

Note 1 : Heteroskedasticity-robust standard errors in parentheses.

2 : *** $p < 0.01$, ** $p < 0.05$, * $p < 0.1$.

Table 7 : Estimation Result (OLS: Expenditure component, State Variables for Financial Networks: 2014, urban area)

VARIABLES	urban area									
	ΔHouse repair	ΔHouse repair	ΔVehicle repair	ΔVehicle repair	Δeducation expense	Δeducation expense	ΔClothing expense	ΔClothing expense	ΔEating outside home	ΔEating outside home
ΔGross revenue	0.0982 (0.0844)	0.0276 (0.0186)	0.0001 (0.0005)	0.0002 (0.0002)	−0.0047** (0.0020)	−0.0005 (0.0017)	−0.0005 (0.0005)	0.0001 (0.0002)	0.0056 (0.0038)	0.0016 (0.0010)
ΔGross revenue × Live outside the house(Child)	−0.0185 (0.0429)		−0.0002 (0.0005)		0.0014 (0.0019)		0.0002 (0.0005)		−0.0029 (0.0023)	
ΔGross revenue × Parents live outside tambon	−0.0111 (0.0197)		−0.0007 (0.0007)		0.0106*** (0.0030)		0.0014*** (0.0005)		0.0010 (0.0017)	
ΔGross Revenue × Own Loan or not	−0.0759 (0.0568)		0.0004 (0.0006)		0.0018 (0.0020)		0.0003 (0.0004)		−0.0029 (0.0026)	
ΔTotal number of household members	15,461.1884 (14,918.3688)	16,449.8612 (14,832.7773)	265.6043 (207.8407)	260.7954 (206.6664)	2,784.8960*** (646.3080)	2,711.9121*** (680.6895)	241.3234 (151.0458)	230.3535 (153.3066)	1,890.5940* (1,111.8933)	1,895.9051* (1,104.6379)
Constant	2,552.6513 (4,307.7015)	1,068.4466 (3,671.8766)	79.2472 (160.7594)	89.0158 (159.3004)	−134.7961 (660.7468)	−107.6723 (665.1395)	189.7026* (111.4536)	195.4946* (112.7906)	1,767.1643*** (500.7169)	1,715.1304*** (503.3583)
Observations	1,422	1,422	1,422	1,422	1,422	1,422	1,422	1,422	1,422	1,422
R-squared	0.0587	0.0272	0.0025	0.0013	0.0184	0.0060	0.0106	0.0022	0.0125	0.0080

Note 1 : Heteroskedasticity-robust standard errors in parentheses.

2 : *** $p<0.01$, ** $p<0.05$, * $p<0.1$.

Chapter 4　Consumption Smoothing in the Aftermath of the 2014 Coup d'état in the Thai Urban and Rural Areas : A Preliminary Estimation

Table 8 : Estimation Result (OLS: Total, State Variables for Financial Networks: 2015)

	rural area	urban area
VARIABLES	ΔTotal expenditure	ΔTotal expenditure
ΔGross revenue	0.0076 (0.0047)	0.0790 (0.0707)
ΔGross revenue × Live outside the house(Child)	−0.0034 (0.0090)	−0.0447 (0.0540)
ΔGross revenue × Parents live outside tambon	0.0003 (0.0048)	−0.0133 (0.0327)
ΔGross Revenue × Own Loan or not	0.0050 (0.0077)	−0.0321 (0.0338)
ΔTotal number of household members	262.6273 (3,061.7717)	22,029.1905 (15,103.4363)
Constant	1,020.3310 (1,795.5093)	3,335.1546 (3,854.7882)
Observations	1,192	1,422
R-squared	0.0131	0.0515

Note 1 : Heteroskedasticity-robust standard errors in parentheses.
　　 2 : *** $p<0.01$, ** $p<0.05$, * $p<0.1$.

Table 9 : Estimation Result (OLS: Expenditure Component, State Variables for Financial Networks: 2015, Rural Area)

	rural area				
VARIABLES	ΔHouse repair	ΔVehicle repair	Δeducation expense	ΔClothing expense	ΔEating outside home
ΔGross revenue	0.0059 (0.0048)	0.0010 (0.0010)	0.0019** (0.0008)	−0.0002 (0.0003)	−0.0010 (0.0010)
ΔGross revenue × Live outside the house(Child)	−0.0014 (0.0098)	−0.0031 (0.0026)	0.0002 (0.0028)	0.0012 (0.0008)	−0.0003 (0.0020)
ΔGross revenue × Parents live outside tambon	−0.0001 (0.0048)	−0.0012 (0.0010)	−0.0003 (0.0010)	0.0005* (0.0003)	0.0013 (0.0010)
ΔGross Revenue × Own Loan or not	0.0047 (0.0095)	0.0020 (0.0022)	−0.0036 (0.0024)	0.0002 (0.0005)	0.0018 (0.0015)
ΔTotal number of household members	−2,492.9574 (2,899.3190)	−247.7548 (232.2058)	1,416.3811** (571.3025)	740.8286*** (152.1250)	846.1298 (868.6655)
Constant	−2,897.3977* (1,675.2010)	−51.2953 (216.2650)	679.2240** (334.5346)	426.2032*** (105.8919)	2,863.5968*** (363.5686)
Observations	1,192	1,192	1,192	1,192	1,192
R-squared	0.0098	0.0121	0.0213	0.0353	0.0041

Note 1 : Heteroskedasticity-robust standard errors in parentheses.
　　 2 : *** $p<0.01$, ** $p<0.05$, * $p<0.1$.

4. Conclusion

　This paper closely followed Kinnan and Townsend (2012) on consumption smoothing against income variations. In order to estimate effects of the Thai 2014 coup d'état on the consumption insurance, we elaborated some changes taking advantage of different data from Kinnan and Townsend (2012). The Household Annual Resurvey 2014 and 2015 provides more detailed information on regional disparities

Table 10 : Estimation Result (OLS: Expenditure Component, State Variables for Financial Networks: 2015, Urban Area)

	urban area				
VARIABLES	ΔHouse repair	ΔVehicle repair	Δeducation expense	ΔClothing expense	ΔEating outside home
ΔGross revenue	0.0765 (0.0701)	−0.0002 (0.0004)	−0.0017 (0.0016)	−0.0002 (0.0005)	0.0046 (0.0032)
ΔGross revenue × Live outside the house(Child)	−0.0404 (0.0535)	0.0005 (0.0005)	0.0004 (0.0020)	−0.0001 (0.0006)	−0.0052* (0.0028)
ΔGross revenue × Parents live outside tambon	−0.0261 (0.0325)	0.0000 (0.0007)	0.0080** (0.0037)	0.0011 (0.0008)	0.0036 (0.0025)
ΔGross Revenue × Own Loan or not	−0.0312 (0.0335)	0.0000 (0.0006)	−0.0014 (0.0019)	0.0004 (0.0005)	−0.0000 (0.0018)
ΔTotal number of household members	16,841.7052 (14,851.0318)	259.2007 (206.2836)	2,772.2244*** (658.2291)	230.0007 (152.9513)	1,926.0595* (1,107.1340)
Constant	1,311.3626 (3,743.3246)	85.6938 (159.6464)	−38.6988 (664.3182)	201.5561* (112.9941)	1,775.2410*** (500.4567)
Observations	1,422	1,422	1,422	1,422	1,422
R-squared	0.0463	0.0020	0.0141	0.0063	0.0156

Note 1 : Heteroskedasticity-robust standard errors in parentheses.
　2 : *** $p < 0.01$, ** $p < 0.05$, * $p < 0.1$.

between rural and urban, and new dummy variables for kinship network and financial access based on Rosenzweig's models and evidence.

The estimation results show that while the urban households are fully insured, the rural ones are not fully insured against income fluctuations. The same spatial feature can be found in each type of expenditures. Among the five items of consumption, co-movements of house repair, education and clothing expenses with the revenue are encountered by the rural households. In the urban cases, on the other hand, we cannot find any types of expenditures positively co-move with revenue. The households in both of urban and rural areas are fully insured in 2015 when influences of the Thai 2014 coup on the nation were stabilized. The effects of financial networks on consumption smoothing are less effective than in the rural area before the 2014 coup. The changes before and after the 2014 coup may be attributed to a policy change in the rice pledge loan scheme, the repayments for the loans which had been deterred before the 2014 coup and was met when the NCPO leader Prayut took office after the coup.

We resolve to take advantage of another variables on risk-sharing between extended family members or with neighbors, from the quite rich data source in the Townsend Thai Project.

References

Chuang, Y., and L. Schechter (2015), "Social Networks in Developing Countries," *Annual Review of Resource Economics,* 7, pp.1-22.

Kinnan, C., and R. Townsend (2012), "Kinship and Financial Networks, Formal Financial Access, and Risk Reduction," *American Economic Review, Papers & Proceedings,* 102(3), pp.289-293.

Kurosaki, T., and Y. Sawada (1999), "Consumption Insurance in Village Economies: Evidence from Pakistan and Other Developing Countries," *Keizai-Kenkyu,* 50(2), pp.155-168 (in Japanese).

Munshi, K. (2011), "Strength in Numbers: Networks as a Solution to Occupational Trap," *Review of Economic Studies,* 78, pp.1069-1101.

Rosenzweig, M. (1988), "Risk, Implicit Contracts and the Family in Rural Areas of Low-Income Countries," *Economic Journal,* 98(393), pp.1148-1170.

Rosenzweig, M., and O. Stark (1989), "Consumption Smoothing, Migration, and Marriage: Evidence from Rural India," *Journal of Political Economy,* 97(4), pp. 905-926.

Samphantharak, K., and R. Townsend (2006), *Households as Corporate Firms,* Cambridge University Press.

Townsend, R. (2016), "Village and Large Economics: The Theory and Measurement of Townsend Thai Project," *Journal of Economic Perspective,* 30(4), pp.199-220.

Townsend, R., and S. Suwanik (2016), "Townsend Thai Household Annual Resurvey Urban and Rural Data Summaries," (http://townsend-thai.mit.edu/data/Urban%20VS%20Rural%20Data%20Summaries_Aug16.pdf).

Townsend, R., S. Sakunthasathien, and R. Jordan (2013), *Chronicles from the Field: The Townsend Thai Project,* The MIT Press.

Townsend Thai Project Household Annual Resurvey: Data Codebook (http://dataverse.harvard.edu/dataverse/rtownsend).

Townsend Thai Project Household Annual Resurvey: Questionnaires (http://dataverse.harvard.edu/dataverse/rtownsend).

Chapter 5

Transactions, Network Centrality, and Foreign Direct Investment As Well As Withdrawal of FDI by Japanese Firms

Shoichi HISA, Yuko HISA, and Hidenobu OKUDA

Abstract

This study[1] shows that FDI firms are generally of large size, have high labor productivity, and have a concentrated network structure. However, the relationships among production network structure, firm size, and productivity are not obvious. On the other hand, withdrawing firms have smaller network concentration than firms performing continuous FDI, however, this is not realized in regression analysis.

We observed the relation between firms and transaction firms: a firm intends to do FDI when a transaction firm does FDI, and the result is similar for withdrawing FDI. This suggests that firms have the tendency of herd behavior regarding FDI, and the network structure affects firms' decision.

JEL : F23, L14, L25

Keywords : Foreign Direct Investment, Transaction Network, Network Structure

1. Introduction

The number or amount of foreign direct investment (FDI) has increased with the background of the stagnation of demand in Japan as well as growth of the economies of developing countries such as those in Asia.

In recent years, the expansion of production for the local market and advancement of the service industry has spread FDI to small businesses. However, as for FDI firms, various risks exist under the current economic conditions of the home country or earnings of the parent company. As a result, even though the problem of withdrawal of FDI occurs, it was not discovered, as it was mostly limited to larger companies and manufacturing companies. In addition, because of data restrictions, few empirical analyses have been conducted.

The analysis on starting FDI is mainly focused on firm productivity. The conventional trade theory supposes the homoscedasticity of firms, while Helpman et al. (2004) consider the heteroscedasticity of firms and theoretically show that high-productivity firms have higher intention to do FDI than small firms. Therefore, in recent years, many researchers have focused on the relation between FDI and firms' productivity. For Japanese firms, Todo (2009) shows that the probability to perform FDI becomes statistically high for productive firms, but the effect is not so large.

---

1 This research has received a research grant from the Japan Society for the Promotion of Science Grants-in-Aid for Scientific Research C (Grant Number: 26380400, Research Representative: Yuko Hisa), for which we would like to express our sincere appreciation.

Chapter 5   Transactions, Network Centrality, and Foreign Direct Investment As Well As Withdrawal of FDI by Japanese Firms   67

On one hand, research on the productivity of Japanese companies has been conducted from the new viewpoint of network analysis. Fujiwara and Aoyama (2011) discusses the relationship between network structure and firm productivity. However, there is little research on the relationship between network structure and FDI or withdrawal from FDI. Itoh and Nakajima (2014) analyze FDI and the network structure of Japanese manufacturing firms to show that high network centrality increases the probability of FDI.

However, in recent years, the problem of withdrawing FDI from abroad has been occurring, but few analyses have verified this. This study analyzes the determinant factors of the withdrawal of FDI from the viewpoint of firms' transaction networks.

In this study, we analyze the herd behavior of firms as regards FDI and withdrawal. When a firm decides the strategy of acquiring information that is not observed easily, its behavior reflects this strategy, and the firms' actions make this information explicit, thus making it available to other firms. Banerjee (1992) and Bikhchandani et al. (1992) theoretically suggest that the mechanism of herd behavior involves acquiring information, and sometimes this behavior leads to a wrong decision. Acemoglu et al. (2011) and Smith and Sorensen (2000) also theoretically discuss the relationship between network structure and herd behavior by focusing on the transition of information through a network. In this study, we analyze herd behavior regarding FDI and withdrawal of FDI in the network structure.

2. Data and the Firm Network of Transaction

In this study, we use three data sets and analyze the characteristics of an FDI firm. First, we use two data sets from the Ministry of Economy, Trade and Industry, namely, the "Basic Survey on Overseas Business Activities" and "Basic Survey of Japanese Business Structure and Activities," to specify the relation between domestic firms and foreign firms (FDI). Next, we use data from the Teikoku Data Bank (TDB) to examine the network structure. We match the three data sets to the 2014 data using ID data. In this analysis, we survey a total of 26,159 firms (manufacturing industry, 11,764 firms; non-manufacturing industry, 19,395 firms).

From TDB data, we realize that 86,805 firms have transacted with firms listed in the "Basic Survey on Overseas Business Activities" in 2012, and 86,569 firms are connected to each other. In this study, 25,383 firms from the "Basic Survey on Overseas Business Activities" are analyzed (Figure 1).

In network analysis, it is important to measure the centrality for each node, and there are several measures of centrality. It is roughly classified into two categories, local and global. Local centrality includes degree assortativity, cluster coefficient, etc. Global centrality includes average path length, closeness, betweenness, eigenvector, etc. (for details, see Masuda and Konno 2010).

The "degree" is the number of the node, and it is equal to the number of transaction companies. However, it is not enough to evaluate the centrality of a firm, because some firms are located on the edge of a network even though there are a large number of transaction firms, these firms do not play a central role in the network. Therefore, in this study, we use the indexes of closeness and betweenness. Closeness

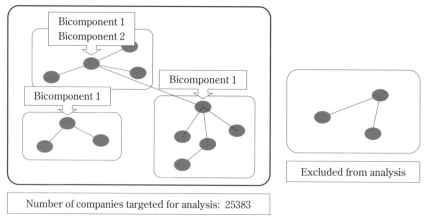

Figure 1 : Transaction Data and Image of the Cut Vertex

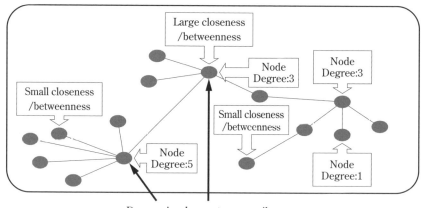

Figure 2 : An Example of Network Centrality

is calculated as the sum of the lengths of the shortest paths between a node and all other nodes in the graph. Thus, the more central a node is, the closer it is to all other nodes. Betweenness for each vertex is the number of shortest paths that pass through the vertex, and high betweenness centrality would have control over the network (for details, see Masuda and Konno 2010). Figure 2 presents an illustration of these indexes.

Table 1 presents the average number of centralities in each industry. It shows that the high-centrality industries include the petroleum-mineral wholesale businesses, oil refineries and textile product wholesale businesses, and nonferrous metal wholesale businesses. From the manufacturing industry, the table includes electrical machinery, apparatus manufacturing for public welfare, boiler-electric motor, etc.

In addition, there is a node at which the network cuts off or a component in the network. Thus, it is possible to say that it plays the important role of joining each inter-network. This is called "the event" (or "the cutting point")[2]. In this study, we specify the firm and set the dummy variable (= 1). However, the firms

---

2 We calculate it using the software Pajek and set component 2. See Nooy et al. (2009) for details.

Table 1 : Rankings in the Higher Rank-Lower Rank Centrality Industry

	Average degree 5 highest-ranking industries	value		Average closeness 5 highest-ranking industries	value
1	Petroleum-mineral wholesale industry	30.46	1	Petroleum refining industry	0.22038
2	Non-ferrous metal wholesale industry	30.37	2	Wholesale textile industry	0.22013
3	Tire and tube manufacturing industry	30.00	3	Heat supply industry	0.21991
4	Petroleum refining industry	28.60	4	Photography industry	0.21748
5	Steel product wholesale industry	28.52	5	Electric industry	0.21632

	Average betweenness 5 highest-ranking industries	value		Average degree 5 lowest-ranking industries Average	value
1	Petroleum-mineral wholesale industry	0.000607516	1	Education	0.13
2	Non-ferrous metal wholesale industry	0.000448334	2	Other entertainment	0.14
3	Petroleum refining industry	0.000343916	3	Security industry	0.18
4	Electronical machinaery and Apparatus manufacturing industry	0.000340846	4	Other restaurant	0.30
5	Boiler/electric motor manufacturing industry	0.000295175	5	Rental industry	0.67

	Average closeness 5 lowest-ranking industries	value		Average betweenness 5 lowest-ranking industries	value
1	Education	0.00254	1	Education	0.00000039
2	Other entertainment	0.00268	2	Security industry	0.00000043
3	Security industry	0.01040	3	Other entertainment	0.00000086
4	Other restaurant	0.01133	4	Other restaurant	0.00000091
5	Rental industry	0.01666	5	Rental industry	0.00000201

in the "Basic Survey on Overseas Business Activities" are of large size, and therefore many companies (18,519 companies) are specified as "the event" (and we defined component 1). Therefore, we created the 1,256-company dummy variable that specified "the event" newly among the event firms, and we defined component 2. Figure 1 shows the image of the event.

There is no difference between the existence and nonexistence of component 1. However, for component 2 firms, firm size, value added, and labor productivity become larger. The reason for excluding companies that deviate from the network is that they are analyzed based on the global centrality index. It is meaningless to compare the use of global indexes by firms that are inside and outside of the network structure.

3. FDI and Network Centrality

We see the relation between the firm size, productivity, and network (Table 2). In manufacturing industries, 2,090 firms do FDI and 9,674 do not in 2017, and in non-manufacturing industries, 1,118 firms do FDI and 13,277 do not. This shows that the rate of firms in the manufacturing industry doing FDI is higher than that for non-manufacturing firms.

In manufacturing industries, the average amount of sales of FDI firms is 75,032 million yen, and that for non-FDI firms is 11,021 million yen. In non-manufacturing industries, the average amount of sales of FDI firms is 116,571 million yen, and that for non-FDI firms is 16,778 million yen. This means that FDI

Table 2 : Main Statistics of Home Companies

Sales(Million Yen)		Mean	Standard Derivation	Median	Max	Min
Manufacturing	Firm Not do FDI	10,211.56	57,938.43	3,126.5	2,680,197	33
	Firm Do FDI	75,032.45	317,939.71	11,416.5	8,241,176	524
Non-Manufacturing	Firm Not do FDI	16,678.92	60,489.09	4,917	2,017,313	144
	Firm Do FDI	116,571.6	559,474.05	17,896.5	10,135,615	241
Labor Productivity (Million Yen)		Mean	Standard Derivation	Median	Max	Min
Manufacturing	Firm Not do FDI	7.78125	6.240814	6.716658	253.334615	−21.034483
	Firm Do FDI	9.664369	5.518193	8.723353	56.223881	−50.439326
Non-Manufacturing	Firm Not do FDI	7.678668	7.253502	6.418182	262.452514	−84.957143
	Firm Do FDI	10.946902	8.380068	9.111602	117.435185	−18.45
Degree		Mean	Standard Derivation	Median	Max	Min
Manufacturing	Firm Not do FDI	10.9908	7.649865	10	245	1
	Firm Do FDI	26.65694	54.77147	13	953	2
Non-Manufacturing	Firm Not do FDI	10.92739	10.84431	10	353	1
	Firm Do FDI	30.38014	64.53686	14	769	1
Closeness		Mean	Standard Derivation	Median	Max	Min
Manufacturing	Firm Not do FDI	0.21457004	0.013751176	0.21552699	0.25804288	0.12642646
	Firm Do FDI	0.22345503	0.014121073	0.22336756	0.28358639	0.17169405
Non-Manufacturing	Firm Not do FDI	0.21609641	0.01454879	0.2178094	0.26092605	0.12663803
	Firm Do FDI	0.22371856	0.015201311	0.22495914	0.29310351	0.16413519
Betweenness		Mean	Standard Derivation	Median	Max	Min
Manufacturing	Firm Not do FDI	4.4162E-05	0.000102631	2.9976E-05	0.0059452	0
	Firm Do FDI	0.00023481	0.001078917	5.1301E-05	0.02543833	0
Non-Manufacturing	Firm Not do FDI	5.3588E-05	0.000224496	2.8869E-05	0.01856298	0
	Firm Do FDI	0.00031507	0.00172615	5.8036E-05	0.03088821	0
Bicomponent 1		Mean	Standard Derivation	Median	Max	Min
Manufacturing	Firm Not do FDI	0.6898904	0.4625622	1	1	0
	Firm Do FDI	0.7555024	0.4298918	1	1	0
Non-Manufacturing	Firm Not do FDI	0.7132635	0.4522544	1	1	0
	Firm Do FDI	0.7119857	0.4530405	1	1	0
Bicomponent 2		Mean	Standard Derivation	Median	Max	Min
Manufacturing	Firm Not do FDI	0.04248501	0.20170335	0	1	0
	Firm Do FDI	0.05311005	0.22430659	0	1	0
Non-Manufacturing	Firm Not do FDI	0.04971002	0.21735339	0	1	0
	Firm Do FDI	0.06618962	0.24872453	0	1	0

firms are larger than non-FDI firms.

Regarding labor productivity (value added / number of employees), the average productivity of FDI firms is 9.66 million yen, and that for non-FDI firms is 7.78 million yen. In non-manufacturing industries, the average amount of sales of FDI firms is 10.947 million yen, and that for non-FDI firms is 7.68 million yen. This means that FDI firms have larger labor productivity than non-FDI firms. Network centrality (degree,

Chapter 5　Transactions, Network Centrality, and Foreign Direct Investment As Well As Withdrawal of FDI by Japanese Firms　71

Table 3 : Correlation Matrix

	Sales (Million Yen)	Labor Productivity (Million Yen)	Degree	Closeness	Betweenness	Bicomponent1	Bicomponent2
Sales (Million Yen)	1.000						
Labor Productivity (Million Yen)	0.149	1.000					
Degree	0.721	0.131	1.000				
Closeness	0.209	0.115	0.318	1.000			
Betweenness	0.708	0.072	0.832	0.217	1.000		
Bicomponent1	−0.010	−0.039	0.004	−0.160	0.004	1.000	
Bicomponent2	0.025	0.016	0.032	0.001	0.020	0.144	1.000

closeness, and betweenness) of FDI firms is larger than that of non-FDI firms. This means that FDI plays a central role in Japan.

Table 3 presents the correlation of variables and shows that the larger is the degree or betweenness, the bigger is the firm size (sales). This suggests that firms with larger sales play a significant role in the transactions within an economy.

4. Analysis of the Relation between FDI and Network Centrality

In this section, we discuss the characteristics of doing FDI and the role of the network structure. We create a dummy variable that is one when firms execute FDI, and zero otherwise. We also analyze it using probit regression analysis (Table 4).

This result shows that manufacturing firms have higher probability of FDI than non-manufacturing firms do, and the larger is the sales or labor productivity of a firm, the higher is the probability of FDI. In addition, high-centrality firms have higher probability of FDI. This shows that under the limitation of firm size and characteristics of the industry, high-centrality firms aggressively do FDI. This may be because firms have the opportunity to acquire information through transactions.

When we analyze a subsidiary firm's performance, manufacturing firms have higher sales than non-manufacturing firms do, and the higher is the parent firm's sales, the larger are the sales of a subsidiary firm. However, high labor productivity of the parent firm results in lower sales of the subsidiary firm. The network centrality of the degree or closeness is significantly positive to sales; however, another centrality is not clearly related to it (Table 5). Labor productivity of the subsidiary firm becomes higher with higher sales size or higher labor productivity of the parent firm, and network centrality is not clearly related to it (Table 6).

From the results, the centrality of a parent firm may not affect the performance of the subsidiary firm.

Table 4 : Result of the FDI by Probit Analysis

Dependent variable: FDI firm $= 1$, otherwise $= 0$ in 2013

	Degree	Closeness	Betweenness	Bicomponent 1	Bicomponent 2
Constant	-1.86 *** [0.02322]	-5.77 *** [0.189]	-1.646 *** [0.02034]	-1.698 *** [0.02675]	-1.61 *** [0.02016]
Industry Dummy (Manufacturing)	0.511 *** [0.0214]	0.538 *** [0.02134]	0.5198 *** [0.02107]	0.5175 *** [0.02093]	0.5175 *** [0.02093]
Sales (Parent firm)	4.299E-08 [0.0000001497]	0.000001461 *** [0.0000001428]	0.00000134 *** [0.0000001737]	0.000002154 *** [0.0000001462]	0.00000213 *** [0.0000001456]
Labor Productivty (Parent firm)	0.01332 *** [0.001455]	0.01186 *** [0.001445]	0.0132 *** [0.001465]	0.01318 *** [0.001473]	0.01297 *** [0.001467]
Network Centrality	0.02168 *** [0.001018]	19.11 *** [0.8566]	752.2 *** [69.81]	0.1269 *** [0.02327]	0.1041 ** [0.04663]

Note : ***, **, and * indicate the 10%, 5%, and 1% significant levels.

Table 5 : Determinants of Subsidiary Sales (by OLS)

Dependent variable: Sales (subsidiary) in 2013

	Degree	Closeness	Betweenness	Bicomponent 1	Bicomponent 2
Constant	$-3,225$ *** [1,910]	$-36,370$ *** [10,310]	-618.6 [1,924]	$-3,548$ [2,293]	$-2,226$ *** [1,903]
Industry Dummy (Manufacturing)	$13,040$ *** [1,573]	$12,820$ *** [1,577]	$12,560$ *** [1,577]	$13,070$ *** [1,588]	$13,170$ *** [1,577]
Sales (Parent firm)	0.009412 *** [0.0007407]	0.009723 *** [0.0006074]	0.01428 *** [0.0007953]	0.01108 *** [0.0004427]	0.01118 *** [0.0004428]
Labor Productivty (Parent firm)	-181.6 * [96.26]	-245.1 ** [97.56]	-274.8 *** [97.77]	-183.4 * [96.59]	-187.3 * [96.35]
Network Centrality	16.71 *** [5.801]	$151,700$ *** [45,270]	$-980,100$ *** [206,300]	$1,562$ [1,767]	$-1,734$ [2,328]

Note : ***, **, and * indicate the 10%, 5%, and 1% significant levels.

Table 6 : Determinants of Subsidiary Labor Productivity (by OLS)

Dependent variable: Labor productivity (subsidiary) in 2013

	Degree	Closeness	Betweenness	Bicomponent 1	Bicomponent 2
Constant	-42.22 ** [17.74]	-47.04 [94.17]	-45.4 ** [17.87]	-43.13 ** [21.01]	-46.94 *** [17.72]
Industry Dummy (Manufacturing)	15 [14.42]	13.27 [14.46]	12.52 [14.46]	14.04 [14.56]	13.03 [14.46]
Sales (Parent firm)	0.00005825 *** [0.000006984]	0.00004531 *** [0.000005681]	0.00004935 *** [0.000007572]	0.00004548 *** [0.000004175]	0.00004541 *** [0.000004181]
Labor Productivty (Parent firm)	4.041 *** [0.9533]	4.032 *** [0.97]	3.941 *** [0.9639]	4.016 *** [0.9544]	4.043 *** [0.9552]
Network Centrality	-0.1237 ** [0.05371]	-1.368 [414.9]	$-1,259$ [1,968]	-5.924 [16.1]	-4.309 [21.35]

Note : ***, **, and * indicate the 10%, 5%, and 1% significant levels.

5. Analysis of FDI Withdrawal

When firms execute FDI in foreign countries, it does not always go favorably. In some cases, firms are forced to withdraw FDI from abroad. Which factors affect the withdrawal of FDI from abroad?

Chapter 5 Transactions, Network Centrality, and Foreign Direct Investment As Well As Withdrawal of FDI by Japanese Firms   73

Table 7 : Regression Analysis by the Probit Model

Dependent variable: Withdrawal of FDI = 1, otherwise = 0 in 2013

	Degree	Closeness	Betweenness	Bicomponent 1	Bicomponent 2
Constant	-1.669 *** [0.03766]	0.2272 [0.27]	-1.706 *** [0.03736]	-1.796 *** [0.05236]	-1.682 *** [0.03765]
Industry Dummy (Manufacturing)	-0.06676 [0.04309]	-0.06215 [0.04318]	-0.06109 [0.04305]	-0.08646 ** [0.04339]	-0.07445 * [0.04301]
Sales (Parent firm)	-0.00000161 ** [0.0000007761]	-0.000001361 [0.0000007236]	-0.000001777 ** [0.0000008088]	-0.000001812 ** [0.000000802]	-0.000001769 ** [0.0000007982]
Sales (Subsidiary firm)	7.255E-08 *** [0.00000001807]	9.247E-08 *** [0.00000001477]	-1.821E-08 [0.0000000219]	1.753E-08 [0.00000001186]	2.361E-08 ** [0.00000001183]
Network Centrality	-0.0005633 *** [0.000163]	-8.435 *** [1.181]	11.96 ** [5.312]	0.1415 *** [0.05172]	-0.1303 * [0.06864]

Note : ***, **, and * indicate the 10%, 5%, and 1% significant levels.

Table 8 : Regression Analysis by the Probit Model

Dependent variable: Withdrawal of FDI = 1, otherwise = 0 in 2013

	Degree	Closeness	Betweenness	Bicomponent 1	Bicomponent 2
Constant	-1.534 *** [0.05503]	-0.4618 ** [0.2305]	-1.582 *** [0.05631]	-1.647 *** [0.06776]	-1.564 *** [0.05447]
Industry Dummy (Manufacturing)	-0.1378 *** [0.04376]	-0.1437 *** [0.04349]	-0.1081 ** [0.04463]	-0.1263 *** [0.04367]	-0.1195 *** [0.04354]
Labor Productivity (Parent firm)	0.00001127 [0.00002441]	0.0000156 [0.00002321]	0.00000469 [0.0000269]	0.000005718 [0.00002704]	0.000006485 [0.00002604]
Labor Productivity (Subsidiary firm)	-0.009358 *** [0.003322]	-0.006804 ** [0.003347]	-0.01009 *** [0.003336]	-0.009988 *** [0.003331]	-0.00989 *** [0.00334]
Network Centrality	-0.0002641 ** [0.0001097]	-4.81 *** [0.993]	2.135 [3.222]	0.1014 * [0.05276]	-0.06492 [0.06955]

Note : ***, **, and * indicate the 10%, 5%, and 1% significant levels.

Tables 7 and 8 present the results of the determinants of FDI withdrawal by probit analysis. The results show that smaller sales size of the subsidiary firm leads to higher probability of withdrawal, and high centrality of the parent firm (high degree or closeness, or component 2 being equal to one) leads to lower probability of withdrawal. However, high betweenness centrality or component 1 being equal to one positively affects withdrawal (Table 7).

Table 8 shows the relationship between labor productivity and FDI withdrawal. It suggests that high labor productivity of the parent firm leads to low probability of withdrawal. However, when looking at network structure, this relationship is not obvious. The degree or closeness has a negative effect on withdrawal, but the component is positively related.

There may be several reasons of withdraw. Sometimes, a firm does not have enough information and fails to conduct FDI with low performance; alternatively, it may have enough information and decide to withdraw in advance to avoid huge loss. Therefore, to understand withdrawal, we should consider the information a firm has.

6. Analysis of FDI, Withdrawal, and Herd Behavior

Acemoglu et al. (2011) and Smith and Sorensen (2000) discuss the relation between network structure and herd behavior. They argue that each agent decides his or her own behavior based on information flowing through the network. Conducting FDI is a risky decision, and if the information available widely is not enough, another behavior may be helpful to make the decision. Tables 9 and 10 present the results of the relationship between the FDI by each country and the transaction firm's behavior. In this analysis, we identify the relationship for each firm and the number of intermediate firms. For example, when a firm transacts directly and does FDI, we set dummy variable distance $1 = 1$. When one firm is mediated and does FDI, distance $2 = 1$, and when two firms are mediated and do FDI, distance $3 = 1$.

Table 9 suggests that the probability of doing FDI becomes high when directly transacting firms do FDI. Especially, when three directly transacting firms execute FDI, the probability becomes high. This means that increasing the number of firms dealing directly induces FDI.

A similar result is observed for withdrawal of FDI (Table 10). Except for India and the Philippines, withdrawal of FDI by transacting firms induces further withdrawal of FDI. This means that the tendency to withdraw strengthens. Then, entry of a non-withdrawing firm makes it difficult for withdrawal to occur. However, the effect is weaker than when doing FDI.

7. Conclusion

In this study, we specified a network structure and analyzed the effects of FDI and withdrawal of FDI. The result suggests that firms doing FDI tend to have large sales, high productivity, and high network centrality; moreover, their degree, closeness, and betweennss are higher than those for non-FDI firms. This means that FDI firms play a central role in the domestic market.

This tendency is observed in probit regression analysis, wherein manufacturing firms have higher probability of FDI than non-manufacturing firms, and high sales or labor productivity of the parent firm leads to FDI. In addition, considering the firm's characteristics or firm size, high-centrality firms tend to do FDI. This means that firms having network centrality, that is, those that play the role of centrality, tend to do FDI positively. This suggests that firms can acquire some information through transactions.

Manufacturing firms are of larger size (sales) than non-manufacturing firms as regards performance of subsidiary FDI firms, and when the parent firm is of large size, the subsidiary firm is also large. Regarding the relation between network centrality and subsidiary firm, degree or closeness is proportional to the subsidiary FDI firm's size, but other network centrality variables are not. For labor productivity of the subsidiary FDI firm, the higher is the parent firms' sales or labor productivity, the larger is the labor productivity of the subsidiary FDI firm.

In addition, for withdrawal of FDI, when the subsidiary FDI firm has small sales, the probability of

Chapter 5   Transactions, Network Centrality, and Foreign Direct Investment As Well As Withdrawal of FDI by Japanese Firms   75

Table 9 : Relation between FDI and Transaction Firms (Probit Model)

Dependent variable: Doing FDI = 1, otherwise = 0 in 2014

		World	USA	INDIA	MALAYSIA	SINGAPORE
	Constant	−5.21078 [54.30856]	−5.684 [94.43]	−8.58295 [395.31831]	−5.83253 [118.14539]	−5.93901 [131.42825]
distance 1	# of FDI = 1 Dummy	0.18226 *** [0.04166]	0.2493 [0.06148]	−0.04132 [0.11141]	0.25637 * [0.10032]	0.2375 ** [0.09023]
	# of FDI = 2 Dummy	0.37872 *** [0.04823]	0.2637 *** [0.1051]	0.17254 [0.1565]	0.3519 * [0.1739]	0.43525 ** [0.14514]
	# of FDI = 3 Dummy	0.83093 *** [0.04432]	0.8055 *** [0.1128]	1.05536 [0.14095]	1.00522 *** [0.18232]	1.02435 *** [0.15013]
distance 2	# of FDI = 1 Dummy	0.19842 [0.29445]	−0.1956 [0.2305]	2.75417 [90.73207]	0.18536 [0.3344]	−0.04229 [0.21615]
	# of FDI = 2 Dummy	0.3988 [0.27186]	0.03373 [0.1923]	3.12707 [90.73182]	0.49472 [0.29732]	0.10313 [0.1951]
	# of FDI = 3 Dummy	0.62957 * [0.23728]	0.3545 * [0.151]	3.575 ** [90.73168]	0.69081 * [0.27638]	0.27618 [0.16286]
distance 3	# of FDI = 1 Dummy	0.01594 [78.60872]	−0.001217 [145.5]	0.21596 [567.53902]	−0.01485 [176.03061]	0.02883 [189.99979]
	# of FDI = 2 Dummy	−0.03361 [89.66717]	−0.0009931 [145.1]	−0.08839 [550.75625]	−0.019 [170.2632]	0.02331 [199.97331]
	# of FDI = 3 Dummy	2.50616 [54.30876]	2.738 [94.43]	2.22317 * [384.76527]	2.26753 [118.142828]	2.77786 [131.42828]
Characteristics of Parents' Fimrm	TFP (Level)	−0.01366 [0.001677]	0.02853 [0.02678]	0.05221 [0.04265]	0.02078 [0.04388]	0.06816 [0.0341]
	Long Term Debt Ratio	0.83051 ** [0.28211]	1.645 ** [0.546]	0.9504 [0.80783]	0.86593 [0.72461]	1.15151 [0.74287]
	Long Term Debt Ratio (Square)	−2.21748 *** [0.48186]	−3.774 ** [1.052]	−2.20787 [1.47072]	−1.60859 [1.19671]	−2.92258 [1.44363]

		THAILAND	INDONESIA	PHILIPPINE	VIETNUM	CHINA
	Constant	−5.48812 [94.018089]	−6.08037 [168.33242]	−6.52626 [232.44968]	−6.074853 [171.58329]	−5.416774 [73.29123]
distance 1	# of FDI = 1 Dummy	0.273993 *** [0.071326]	0.31481 *** [0.09052]	0.173 [0.13724]	0.307291 ** [0.100815]	0.14667 ** [0.046385]
	# of FDI = 2 Dummy	0.490996 *** [0.104065]	0.37623 * [0.16487]	0.43106 [0.26603]	0.557092 *** [0.146056]	0.32628 *** [0.06171]
	# of FDI = 3 Dummy	1.025165 *** [0.126538]	1.25241 *** [0.17284]	0.83838 * [0.42401]	1.097726 *** [0.200269]	0.699855 *** [0.065671]
distance 2	# of FDI = 1 Dummy	−0.284692 [0.347812]	0.24492 [0.24082]	0.30629 [0.31074]	0.297801 [0.241386]	0.2839 [0.258255]
	# of FDI = 2 Dummy	0.21955 [0.246822]	0.35051 [0.23639]	0.53224 [0.29565]	0.162788 [0.263266]	0.420912 [0.248366]
	# of FDI = 3 Dummy	0.51268 * [0.214466]	0.64624 ** [0.20787]	0.89387 ** [0.2738]	0.530201 [0.209912]	0.638225 ** [0.217389]
distance 3	# of FDI = 1 Dummy	−0.005824 [135.164925]	−0.02211 [240.72761]	−0.09807 [328.7503]	−0.006908 [256.803621]	−0.003134 [109.183961]
	# of FDI = 2 Dummy	−0.018511 [136.335622]	−0.02812 [232.43904]	−0.26436 [312.02133]	−0.021685 [254.473727]	−0.075198 [114.596374]
	# of FDI = 3 Dummy	2.4313255 [94.018283]	2.59517 [168.33247]	2.52529 [232.44969]	2.573035 [171.586386]	2.529486 [73.291442]
Characteristics of Parents' Fimrm	TFP (Level)	−0.037643 [0.034064]	0.04449 [0.0394]	0.11633 * [0.05047]	0.030019 [0.043545]	0.014522 [0.02053]
	Long Term Debt Ratio	0.918612 [0.595638]	1.32265 [0.73262]	1.42629 [0.9484]	1.970134 [0.890214]	1.293554 *** [0.361587]
	Long Term Debt Ratio (Square)	−2.50156 * [1.100069]	−2.64422 [1.32174]	−1.91537 [1.52251]	−4.184515 [1.745856]	−2.874765 [0.637712]

Note : ***, **, * and indicate the significance levels of 0.1%, 1%, 5%, and 10%.

Table 10 : Withdrawal of FDI and the Transacted Behavior Effect (Probit Model)

Dependent variable: Withdrawal of FDI = 1, otherwise = 0 in 2014

		World	USA	INDIA	MALAYSIA	SINGAPORE
	Constant	−5.182694	−5.51857	−3.08948 ***	−5.894	−5.800842
		[56.249002]	[94.12379]	[0.41774]	[150.3]	[166.740039]
distance 1	# of FDI = 1 Dummy	0.159795 *** [0.041114]	0.02203 [0.07805]	0.19244 [0.21744]	0.2624 [0.1386]	0.089598 [0.120805]
	# of FDI = 2 Dummy	0.380764 *** [0.047705]	0.38251 *** [0.09311]	0.50498 [0.39708]	0.3774 [0.362]	0.007949 [0.341734]
	# of FDI = 3 Dummy	0.786606 *** [0.045416]	0.86726 *** [0.09634]	−3.64578 [2633.10092]	1.682 *** [0.4122]	1.955066 *** [0.24494]
distance 2	# of FDI = 1 Dummy	0.206112 [0.287133]	0.12646 [0.35345]	0.69095 [0.5127]	0.0007909 [0.2709]	0.351528 [0.230717]
	# of FDI = 2 Dummy	0.218323 [0.279679]	0.40793 [0.32127]	−2.75081 [236.58234]	−0.2041 [0.3324]	0.448427 *** [0.228772]
	# of FDI = 3 Dummy	0.596946 * [0.238575]	0.67734 * [0.29155]	1.47448 ** [0.50778]	0.525 * [0.2076]	0.673274 ** [0.205956]
distance 3	# of FDI = 1 Dummy	−0.002548 [81.235917]	−0.02798 [146.05536]	−4.3741 [638.37952]	3.264 [150.3]	−0.078024 [231.629777]
	# of FDI = 2 Dummy	−0.070197 [89.574773]	−0.06929 [146.41684]	−4.57282 [448.52438]	−0.02143 [201.7]	−0.117542 [223.167365]
	# of FDI = 3 Dummy	2.529042 [56.249361]	2.27507 [94.12418]	−1.30511 * [0.53217]	2.501 [150.3]	2.473463 [166.740109]
Characteristics of Parents' Firm	TFP (Level)	−0.014695 [0.016543]	−0.06238 [0.03461]	0.05329 [0.07882]	−0.01652 [0.06466]	−0.067943 [0.054121]
	Long Term Debt Ratio	0.833004 ** [0.280713]	1.69926 ** [0.61728]	1.35849 [1.30726]	0.6072 [1.007]	0.831116 [0.884899]
	Long Term Debt Ratio (Square)	−2.187758 ** [0.478727]	−3.76479 ** [1.16811]	−1.97093 [2.11718]	−1.346 [1.678]	−2.131795 [1.606557]

		THAILAND	INDONESIA	PHILIPPINE	VIETNAM	CHINA
	Constant	−5.72894	−6.088567	−3.101 ***	−6.298465	−5.551022
		[121.319575]	[207.097834]	[0.3966]	[274.397609]	[105.362817]
distance 1	# of FDI = 1 Dummy	0.338971 *** [0.085169]	0.411386 ** [0.136346]	−0.01245 [0.2403]	0.502814 ** [0.194497]	0.206546 *** [0.059515]
	# of FDI = 2 Dummy	0.357951 * [0.165273]	0.765296 *** [0.215309]	0.3925 [0.3756]	1.237801 *** [0.342658]	0.413059 *** [0.083524]
	# of FDI = 3 Dummy	1.00288 *** [0.188743]	−3.2706 [561.130832]	−3.118 [587.5]	1.95611 ** [0.648871]	0.817501 *** [0.090824]
distance 2	# of FDI = 1 Dummy	0.007142 [0.217667]	0.214226 [0.242516]	0.1697 [0.2098]	0.088208 [0.228414]	0.183483 [0.214932]
	# of FDI = 2 Dummy	−0.04842 [0.235371]	0.329659 [0.235895]	−0.1244 [0.3102]	−0.081634 [0.315264]	0.446832 * [0.203742]
	# of FDI = 3 Dummy	0.521011 ** [0.171738]	0.696896 *** [0.205693]	0.4971 ** [0.1926]	0.622665 *** [0.185144]	0.451703 * [0.184868]
distance 3	# of FDI = 1 Dummy	−0.00858 [173.576845]	−0.006947 [302.070511]	0.0002151 [0.474]	−0.006032 [373.783821]	−0.004185 [151.681827]
	# of FDI = 2 Dummy	3.173822 [121.320013]	−0.166044 [274.844477]	−3.36 [174.6]	−0.074806 [353.812036]	−0.012252 [156.454197]
	# of FDI = 3 Dummy	2.549536 [121.319639]	2.607252 [207.097815]	−0.6101 [0.3687]	2.773443 [274.39757]	2.657632 [105.362923]
Characteristics of Parents' Firm	TFP (Level)	−0.040669 [0.041978]	−0.046351 [0.064372]	−0.004088 [0.07391]	−0.011437 [0.076743]	−0.019121 [0.02313]
	Long Term Debt Ratio	0.776757 [0.587687]	1.290572 [1.089975]	2.137 * [1.063]	0.915702 [1.190817]	0.406728 [0.368294]
	Long Term Debt Ratio (Square)	−1.168877 [0.901356]	−2.862313 [2.029782]	−2.109 [1.436]	−1.407813 [1.90337]	−0.81289 [0.547287]

Note : ***, **, * and indicate the significance levels of 0.1%, 1%, 5%, and 10%.

withdrawing FDI becomes high, and when the parent firm has high labor productivity, the probability of withdrawing is low. For the network centrality of the parent firm, degree and closeness are negatively correlated with withdrawal, while betweenness or component 1 is positively related to withdrawal.

Herd behavior is observed in both performing FDI and withdrawing FDI, and this implies the existence of a relationship between the decision to conduct FDI and the network structure.

References

Acemoglu, D., A. Ozdaglar, and A. P. Gheibi (2011), "Bayesian Learning in Social Networks," *Review of Economic Studies,* 78, pp.1201-1236.

Banerjee, A. V. (1992), "A Simple Model of Herd Behavior," *Quarterly Journal of Economics,* 107, pp.797-817.

Bikhchandani, S., D. Hirshleifer, and I. Welch (1992), "A Theory of Fads, Fashion, Custom, and Cultural Change as Information Cascade," *Journal of Political Economy,* 100, pp.992-1026.

Fujiwara, Y., and H. Aoyama (2011), "Stochastic Origin of Scaling Laws in Productivity and Employment." RIETI Discussion Paper Series, 11-E-044.

Helpman, E., M. M. Melitz, and S. R. Yaeple (2004), "Export Versus FDI with Heterogeneous Firms," *American Economic Review,* 94, pp.300-316.

Itoh, R., and K. Nakajima (2014), "Impact of Supply Chain Network Structure on FDI; Theory and Evidence," RIETI Discussion Paper Series, 14-E-027.

Masuda, N., and N. Konno (2010), *The Complicated Network from the Basics to the Advance, Fukuzatsu Network Kiso kara Ouyou made*, Kindai Kagaku Sha (in Japanese).

Nooy, W. De, A. Mrvar, and V. Batagelj (2009), *Exploratory Social Network Analysis with Pajek,* Tokyo Denki University Press (in Japanese).

Smith, L., and P. Sorensen (2000), "Pathological Outcomes of Observational Lerning," *Econometrica,* 68, pp.371-398.

Todo, Y. (2009), "Quantitative Evaluation of Determinants of Export and FDI: Firm-Level Evidence from Japan". RIETI Discussion Paper Series, 09-E-019.

Chapter 6

Dynamics of the Network Structure and Activity of Japanese Firms

Yuko HISA, and Shoichi HISA

Abstract

In this study, we analyze transaction data, measure the centrality of each firm, and trace over several years (1996, 2002, 2007, 2010, and 2013). There are several indices including degree, closeness, betweenness, and the degree (number of transaction firms) and betweenness (degree of bridging or controlling by the flow on the network) are highly and positively related to firm size, sales, and number of employees. This means that firms that play a significant role in the trading network tend to be large in size.

For the centrality of each firm, existing for long periods (1996-2013) increased centrality, and it is possible that the phenomenon called "Matthew's law" exists in network-theory.

JEL : D22, L14, L25

Keywords : Transaction Network, Matthews' Law, Centrality

1. Introduction

This study discusses the transaction of firms in relation with the network structure. The network is an element of social structure; however, it is very difficult to grasp and analyze all the features of the network.

Takayasu et al. (2007) and Ohnishi et al. (2010) analyze the transactions of firms and network structure from the perspective of economics. They showed that the histogram of the degree of firms' transactions reflects the power law, and they have a scale-free network. Scale free means that the network is focused on a particular firm and is huge. The authors show that degree distribution depends on the power law with 1.4 and is scale free. In addition, it clarifies that in a small-world network, the average number of nodes that intervene between the shortest path among the arbitrary nodes between two firms with a strongly connected component is small compared with the network size.

In this study, we analyze the transition of a firms' network in a time series. There are several indexes of centrality, which indicate the characteristics of a firm's position in the whole network, and we specify their relations with firm characteristics.

According to Hisa et al. (2016), measuring the average of centrality-degree, closeness, and betweenness-industries with high centrality include the petroleum-mineral wholesale businesses, oil refinery and textile product wholesale businesses, and nonferrous metal wholesale businesses. For the manufacturing industry, the businesses involve electrical machinery, apparatus manufacturing for the public welfare, boiler- electric motor, etc. For the degree, petroleum-mineral wholesale businesses, nonferrous metal wholesale businesses, tire-tube manufacturing, oil refining, and steel product wholesale businesses are the top five industries, and for closeness, these include oil refining, textile product wholesale businesses, heat supply industry, photography business, and electric utility industry. For betweenenss, the top industries are the petroleum-mineral wholesale businesses, nonferrous metal wholesale businesses, oil refining, electrical machinery and apparatus manufacturing for the public welfare, and boiler-motor manufacturing. These results show that the heat supply industry, photography business, and electric utility industry are tertiary industries, and f the other indexes have different values, except for the non-manufacturing industry. We consider the above and analyze the relation between network centrality and firm characteristics.

Firms' transactions change in a time series. Goto et al. (2015) suggest that, over the past 20 years, fluctuation in the number of companies (number of nodes) is fairly steady at six, and the ratio of start-ups, bankrupt firms, and firms created through mergers and acquisitions is 5:3:2. Although, it is approximately regular, the total number (link count) of dealings clarify that it is possible that every year about 15% of the dealings disappear or change. In this study, we analyze the changes in the transition of firms from the perspective of firms.

2. Data

In this study, the analysis is based on data from the Teikoku Data Bank. Transaction data of the analyzed firms are processed over several years (1996, 2002, 2007, 2010, and 2013); a total of 27,647 companies firms were analyzed that have equal to or more than 50 employees and more than 30 million yen as capital based on the "Business Activity Data Survey" for 2013. As these firms changed their trading partners and network structure, finally, 139,075 firms were analyzed.

In the network analysis, it is important to measure the centrality for each node, and there are several measures of centrality. These were roughly classified into two categories: local and global. Local centrality includes the degree, assortativity, cluster coefficient, etc. Global centrality includes the average path length, closeness, betweenness, eigenvector, etc. (for details, see Masuda and Konno 2010). The latter index is calculated using information for the whole network, and it is meaningful to capture a position of each firm in the network structure.

The "degree" is the number of the node, and it is equal to the number of transaction companies. However, it is not enough to evaluate the centrality of a firm, because some firms are located on the edge of a network even though the number of transaction firms is high. These firms do not play a central role in the network. Therefore, in this study, we use the indexes of closeness and betweenness. Closeness is calculated as the sum of the lengths of the shortest paths between a node and all other nodes in the graph. Thus, the more central a node is, the closer it is to all other nodes. Betweenness for each vertex is the number of shortest paths that pass through the vertex, and high betweenness centrality would have control over the network (for details, see Masuda and Konno 2010). The reason for using these indexes is that betweenness does not become large even though the degree is large. That is, betweenness become small (or large) in some cases when the degree is large (or small). In the following analysis, we estimate the degree, closeness, and betweenness and analyze them.

In addition, there are information on "purchase" (in) and "sale" (out) in the transaction data. We analyze the index of degree and closeness separately by analyzing purchase (in), sale (out), and "no distinction between in and out" (all). Moreover, betweennness only considers "no distinction between in and out" (all).

3. Main Statistics

The main statistics of the degree, closeness, and betweenness of firm in data during 1996, 2002, 2007, 2010, and 2013 are as follows. There are 12,876 firms existing during 1996-2013. For the degree, the average of number of purchasing firms (in-degree) is 6-8, and the maximum number is 393-537. The minimum value 0 indicates the non-recognition of a purchasing firm, although some transactions are carried out. The median is 5, and the firms purchase from 5 firms on average (Table 1. 1). The number of sales firms is 6-8 on average, and median is 5 for purchasing (out-degree; Table 1. 2). Regarding the number of transition firms (both purchasing and sales), the median is 10 and the average is 11-17 (all; Table 1. 3).

The average is bigger than the median value because the distribution is left-skewed. The transition

Table 1. 1 : Degree (IN) : Network Index of Purchasing (1996-2013)

	Degree IN 1996	Degree IN 2002	Degree IN 2007	Degree IN 2010	Degree IN 2013
Mean	5.785337	6.425054	6.856322	7.601895	8.707751
Variance	11.64179	12.73078	12.66406	14.33417	16.96887
Maximum	393	395	436	456	537
Minimum	0	0	0	0	0
Median	5	5	5	5	5
First Quartile	4	5	5	5	5
Third Quartile	6	6	6	7	8
Sample Size	12,876	12,876	12,876	12,876	12,876

Table 1. 2 : Degree (OUT) : Network Index of Sales (1996-2013)

	Degree OUT 1996	Degree OUT 2002	Degree OUT 2007	Degree OUT 2010	Degree OUT 2013
Mean	5.646785	6.313995	6.803821	7.498913	8.674278
Variance	14.48134	14.48383	13.97368	14.39688	16.98948
Maximum	803	779	763	564	499
Minimum	0	0	0	0	0
Median	5	5	5	5	6
First Quartile	3	4	4	5	5
Third Quartile	6	6	7	7	8
Sample Size	12,876	12,876	12,876	12,876	12,876

Chapter 6 Dynamics of the Network Structure and Activity of Japanese Firms   81

data show that few firms have a large number of transactions

Closeness of purchasing (IN, Table 2. 1) is 0.1-0.2 on average, and the maximum is 1.6-1.7. The median is 1.1-1.2. Here, 0 means non-recognition of a purchasing firm. For the closeness of purchasing (OUT, Table 2. 2), the average is 0.09-0.1 and median is 0.1. For the closeness of transition (ALL, Table 2. 3), the median and average are similar at 0.22.

Betweenness is 0.0001 on average, and the maximum is 0.03-0.06. The median is 0.00003~0.00005 and larger than average (Table 3).

Moreover, the elementary statistics about the sales (1 million yen of units) and number of employees (Table 4. 1 and Table 4. 2, respectively) indicating the size of the business are as follows. The main statistics of sales (unit: one million yen) and the number of employees (Table 4. 1 and 4. 2) are as follows. The tables

Table 1. 3 : Degree (ALL) : Network Index of Transaction Firms (1996-2013)

	Degree ALL 1996	Degree ALL 2002	Degree ALL 2007	Degree ALL 2010	Degree ALL 2013
Mean	11.43212	12.73905	13.66014	15.10081	17.38203
Variance	24.27104	25.39734	24.62993	26.46102	31.31439
Maximum	1,185	1,174	1,137	848	916
Minimum	1	1	1	1	1
Median	10	10	10	11	12
First Quartile	7	8	9	10	10
Third Quartile	11	12	13	14	16
Sample Size	12,876	12,876	12,876	12,876	12,876

Table 2. 1 : Closeness (IN) : Network Index of Purchasing (1996-2013)

	Closeness IN 1996	Closeness IN 2002	Closeness IN 2007	Closeness IN 2010	Closeness IN 2013
Mean	0.102578	0.110504	0.108945	0.115636	0.124868
Variance	0.034094	0.031867	0.029198	0.026125	0.021091
Maximum	0.158728	0.163207	0.160941	0.17033	0.179721
Minimum	0	0	0	0	0
Median	0.111481	0.117947	0.114961	0.119954	0.127211
First Quartile	0.101229	0.1091	0.10694	0.112548	0.11985
Third Quartile	0.120547	0.126102	0.123027	0.127889	0.135071
Sample Size	12,876	12,876	12,876	12,876	12,876

Table 2. 2 : Closeness (OUT) : Network Index of Sales (1996-2013)

	Closeness OUT 1996	Closeness OUT 2002	Closeness OUT 2007	Closeness OUT 2010	Closeness OUT 2013
Mean	0.093134	0.099816	0.09813	0.102447	0.107818
Variance	0.048053	0.033702	0.033142	0.029198	0.023313
Maximum	0.187296	0.175777	0.17361	0.170843	0.170608
Minimum	0	0	0	0	0
Median	0.109565	0.107717	0.106796	0.108935	0.111579
First Quartile	0.087364	0.088644	0.089192	0.094229	0.098984
Third Quartile	0.125837	0.121312	0.118789	0.120267	0.121515
Sample Size	12,876	12,876	12,876	12,876	12,876

Table 2. 3 : Closeness (ALL) : Network Index of Transition (1996-2013)

	Closeness ALL 1996	Closeness ALL 2002	Closeness ALL 2007	Closeness ALL 2010	Closeness ALL 2013
Mean	0.220763	0.218928	0.216443	0.218311	0.221696
Variance	0.023228	0.019315	0.017997	0.016144	0.014102
Maximum	0.312781	0.303468	0.300278	0.293725	0.294792
Minimum	4.56E-05	3.63E-05	3.18E-05	2.86E-05	2.41E-05
Median	0.222458	0.220565	0.218072	0.219417	0.22216
First Quartile	0.208497	0.208847	0.207134	0.209845	0.213608
Third Quartile	0.235685	0.231603	0.228206	0.228783	0.230608
Sample Size	12,876	12,876	12,876	12,876	12,876

Table 3 : Betweenness (ALL) : Network Index of Transition (1996-2013)

	Betweenness ALL 1996	Betweenness ALL 2002	Betweenness ALL 2007	Betweenness ALL 2010	Betweenness ALL 2013
Mean	0.0001238	0.0001258	0.0001251	0.0001173	0.0001117
Variance	0.0009695	0.0009381	0.0009036	0.0007416	0.0007049
Maximum	0.0634181	0.0648388	0.0632333	0.0402449	0.0297491
Minimum	0	0	0	0	0
Median	0.000057	0.000053	0.000048	0.000044	0.000038
First Quartile	0.000019	0.000026	0.000024	0.000024	0.000022
Third Quartile	0.000095	0.000091	0.000087	0.000080	0.000070
Sample Size	12,876	12,876	12,876	12,876	12,876

Table 4. 1 : Main Statistics of Sales

	Sales 1996	Sales 2002	Sales 2007	Sales 2010	Sales 2013
Mean	35,033.231	25,572.213	39,187.241	32,747.65	35,502.36
Variance	347,863.8	190,107.49	270,224.73	197,838.78	222,206.99
Maximum	15,491,757	9,301,198	11,571,834	8,597,873	10,135,615
Minimum	159	25	222	203	33
Median	6,724	5,590	7,138	6,116	6,576
First Quartile	3,165	2,580	3,172	2,662	2,881.5
Third Quartile	16,537.5	13,952	18,174	15,923.5	17,427.75
Sample Size	11,155	11,709	11,709	12,183	12,388

Table 4. 2 : Main Statistics of Employment

	Employee 1996	Employee 2002	Employee 2007	Employee 2010	Employee 2013
Mean	529.65522	429.59604	533.99283	554.27924	567.84307
Variance	21,74.0361	1,573.4915	2,020.0463	2,025.3954	2,066.159
Maximum	76,106	70,300	80,300	76,130	76,840
Minimum	50	50	50	50	50
Median	180	158	171	171	170
First Quartile	107	91	100	97	96
Third Quartile	375	324	361	368	366
Sample Size	11,155	11,709	11,709	12,183	12,388

Chapter 6   Dynamics of the Network Structure and Activity of Japanese Firms   83

show that mean is larger than median left-skewed distribution. In addition, sales have largely decreased in 2002.

How is the centrality related to firm size, sales, or employees? Table 5 shows the correlation of sales or employees and their degree, closeness, and betweenness (1996-2013). Among the degrees of in, out, and all, the in-degree is highly correlated to firm size. The out-degree is highly correlated to sales, but not to employees. This result may be reflected on the differences in the industry. In the data, the final demand as an individual customer is not identified, and therefore the out-degree becomes small even though the sales are large as it is a retail industry.

Table 5 : Correlation of Degree, Sales, and Employees

	In-degree 1996	In-degree 2002	In-degree 2007	In-degree 2010	In-degree 2013
Sales 1996	0.725	0.682	0.626	0.597	0.555
Sales 2002	−0.001	−0.003	−0.005	−0.004	−0.005
Sales 2007	0.736	0.739	0.730	0.723	0.693
Sales 2010	0.708	0.721	0.721	0.741	0.727
Sales 2013	0.672	0.677	0.671	0.690	0.686
Employee 1996	0.748	0.780	0.784	0.825	0.816
Employee 2002	−0.005	−0.008	−0.008	−0.005	−0.006
Employee 2007	0.642	0.699	0.736	0.778	0.767
Employee 2010	0.605	0.664	0.702	0.745	0.737
Employee 2013	0.587	0.646	0.685	0.743	0.742

	Out-degree 1996	Out-degree 2002	Out-degree 2007	Out-degree 2010	Out-degree 2013
Sales 1996	0.895	0.855	0.785	0.750	0.670
Sales 2002	0.001	0.001	0.000	0.004	0.004
Sales 2007	0.767	0.780	0.764	0.765	0.726
Sales 2010	0.666	0.691	0.681	0.720	0.712
Sales 2013	0.665	0.680	0.663	0.707	0.708
Employee 1996	0.327	0.412	0.426	0.478	0.486
Employee 2002	0.001	0.000	−0.001	0.002	0.002
Employee 2007	0.265	0.342	0.369	0.422	0.434
Employee 2010	0.248	0.320	0.346	0.396	0.408
Employee 2013	0.243	0.313	0.337	0.394	0.412

	Degree 1996	Degree 2002	Degree 2007	Degree 2010	Degree 2013
Sales 1996	0.882	0.829	0.766	0.730	0.663
Sales 2002	0.000	−0.001	−0.002	0.000	−0.001
Sales 2007	0.811	0.815	0.809	0.807	0.769
Sales 2010	0.737	0.755	0.757	0.793	0.780
Sales 2013	0.719	0.727	0.721	0.759	0.756
Employee 1996	0.552	0.624	0.642	0.705	0.704
Employee 2002	−0.002	−0.004	−0.004	−0.002	−0.002
Employee 2007	0.466	0.545	0.588	0.651	0.651
Employee 2010	0.438	0.515	0.557	0.619	0.620
Employee 2013	0.427	0.502	0.544	0.617	0.626

Note : Regarding the part in gray, the coefficient of correlation is equal to or more than 0.6.

Table 6 shows that firm size does not seem to be correlated to closeness. This result suggests that firm size is not related to short distance to all the firms (number of intermediate firm) in the network structure; that is, it is not necessary for a large firm to shorten its distance to all firms in the whole network.

If a firm acquires information about transaction firms, firms with high closeness can easily obtain more information. In this case, firms with high closeness may bring advantages for other firms. For example, when conducting credit transactions for sales or purchase, high closeness can more easily avoid loss when another firm becomes bankrupt.

Table 6 : Correlation of Closeness, Sales, and Employees

	Closeness (IN) 1996	Closeness (IN) 2002	Closeness (IN) 2007	Closeness (IN) 2010	Closeness (IN) 2013
Sales 1996	0.082	0.077	0.075	0.088	0.100
Sales 2002	0.005	0.007	−0.015	−0.005	−0.006
Sales 2007	0.088	0.094	0.105	0.117	0.135
Sales 2010	0.092	0.098	0.104	0.133	0.145
Sales 2013	0.087	0.092	0.096	0.118	0.140
Employee 1996	0.114	0.110	0.111	0.130	0.148
Employee 2002	0.009	0.002	−0.009	0.000	−0.008
Employee 2007	0.097	0.110	0.124	0.138	0.158
Employee 2010	0.091	0.109	0.116	0.144	0.158
Employee 2013	0.091	0.108	0.115	0.136	0.159

	Closeness (OUT) 1996	Closeness (OUT) 2002	Closeness (OUT) 2007	Closeness (OUT) 2010	Closeness (OUT) 2013
Sales 1996	0.062	0.072	0.074	0.082	0.094
Sales 2002	0.002	0.008	−0.007	0.011	0.011
Sales 2007	0.068	0.083	0.088	0.100	0.116
Sales 2010	0.058	0.076	0.082	0.098	0.115
Sales 2013	0.060	0.076	0.082	0.096	0.116
Employee 1996	0.044	0.063	0.065	0.079	0.096
Employee 2002	0.010	0.008	0.000	0.006	0.007
Employee 2007	−0.002	0.021	0.025	0.045	0.067
Employee 2010	−0.016	0.007	0.011	0.033	0.055
Employee 2013	−0.024	−0.003	0.003	0.024	0.053

	Closeness (ALL) 1996	Closeness (ALL) 2002	Closeness (ALL) 2007	Closeness (ALL) 2010	Closeness (ALL) 2013
Sales 1996	0.147	0.159	0.164	0.187	0.208
Sales 2002	0.013	0.012	−0.014	−0.004	0.000
Sales 2007	0.158	0.188	0.211	0.234	0.261
Sales 2010	0.158	0.189	0.208	0.252	0.274
Sales 2013	0.152	0.181	0.197	0.233	0.266
Employee 1996	0.171	0.196	0.206	0.240	0.273
Employee 2002	0.014	0.012	−0.002	0.005	0.004
Employee 2007	0.134	0.179	0.215	0.244	0.277
Employee 2010	0.122	0.169	0.198	0.246	0.272
Employee 2013	0.117	0.163	0.191	0.231	0.273

However, as the financial system has worked well systematically, acquiring information and financial statements of the transaction firms is not necessary. Thus, in this analysis, for expanding firm size, high closeness is not necessary.

Table 7 shows the relationship of betweenness with firm size, and sales are highly correlated to betweenness. Betweenness means bridging or controlling the flow of the network, and large firms may control goods or services in the whole network.

In addition, Table 8 shows the relations of auto-correlation and correlation between the sales and employees, and the correlation is positively related.

Table 7 : Correlation of Betweenness, Sales, and Employees

	Betweenness (ALL) 1996	Betweenness (ALL) 2002	Betweenness (ALL) 2007	Betweenness (ALL) 2010	Betweenness (ALL) 2013
Sales 1996	0.884	0.860	0.812	0.855	0.774
Sales 2002	−0.002	−0.002	−0.004	−0.003	−0.003
Sales 2007	0.774	0.795	0.805	0.848	0.832
Sales 2010	0.680	0.681	0.695	0.778	0.798
Sales 2013	0.679	0.669	0.672	0.759	0.808
Employee 1996	0.398	0.425	0.467	0.547	0.557
Employee 2002	−0.003	−0.004	−0.006	−0.006	−0.005
Employee 2007	0.315	0.352	0.404	0.482	0.489
Employee 2010	0.300	0.333	0.379	0.457	0.464
Employee 2013	0.295	0.330	0.373	0.461	0.479

Note : Regarding the part in gray, the coefficient of correlation is equal to or more than 0.6.

Table 8 : Coefficient of Correlation between Sales and Number of Employees

	Sales 1996	Sales 2002	Sales 2007	Sales 2010	Sales 2013
Sales 1996	1.000				
Sales 2002	−0.004	1.000			
Sales 2007	0.858	−0.003	1.000		
Sales 2010	0.789	−0.003	0.969	1.000	
Sales 2013	0.778	−0.003	0.951	0.982	1.000
Employee 1996	0.448	−0.004	0.604	0.650	0.590
Employee 2002	−0.005	0.586	−0.005	−0.005	−0.004
Employee 2007	0.409	−0.005	0.617	0.675	0.611
Employee 2010	0.393	−0.006	0.601	0.652	0.599
Employee 2013	0.395	−0.005	0.601	0.662	0.599

	Employee 1996	Employee 2002	Employee 2007	Employee 2010	Employee 2013
Employee 1996	1.000				
Employee 2002	−0.005	1.000			
Employee 2007	0.916	−0.006	1.000		
Employee 2010	0.899	−0.006	0.979	1.000	
Employee 2013	0.882	−0.005	0.967	0.987	1.000

Note : Regarding the part in gray, the coefficient of correlation is equal to or more than 0.6.

4. Transition of the Network Structure in the Time Series

Does the structure of the network change over time? Whether or not the network structure changes depends on the competitive environment in the market economy. In the market economy, income and sales are concentrated on few individual or firms, and previous studies suggest that this relates to the network structure. That is, the network structure may be highly related to the income or asset gap and the difference in firm size; this is the reason why many researchers focus on studying the network structure.

On the contrary, even though the market mechanism induces inequality of individuals or firms, it is significant and important to work the principle of competition well and guarantee the opportunities of success and expansion of firm size, thus bringing efficiency to the economy. In fact, some large firms withdraw from market because of huge loss; alternatively, they shrink or become bankrupt. In contrast, other small firms grow and turn into a large company. That is, the reason for accepting inequality to some extent is that competition induces social mobility. In this study, we plotted the centrality in two dimensions for the previous year and next year, and high-centrality firms transit after several years.

However, according to the market mechanism, an effort is rewarded by, on one hand, the element of competition that invents a gap at the individual and company levels and, on the other hand, the guaranteed opportunity to expand the size of the business, which are both important for ensuring efficiency. Indeed, when considering companies, for large-scale businesses, the financial status worsens and the size of business reduces, and they may withdraw from the market due to bankruptcy; however, in some cases, small businesses rise up, grow, and become big businesses. In other words, it is possible that social mobility happens due to the element of competition working in the market and tolerating a certain degree of disparity in the market mechanism. Below, we attempt to see whether the centrality of each company changes in time by plotting centrality between the previous and next investigation years on a correlation chart in two dimensions. The analysis shows how the centrality of a big company changes over several years.

The larger the number of purchasing firms (in-degree: Figure 1) is in the previous year, the larger it probably becomes in the next year. In the figure, the diagonal straight line is drawn at 45 degrees, which increases when a plot is over the line. This suggests that there are more firms over the 45-degree line than down the 45-degree, and many firms intend to increase their purchasing. However, in 2002-2007, the results seems to be reverse.

The number of sales (out-degree) showed a similar result (Figure 2). Higher number of sales leads to increase in sales in the next year. Here, there are many companies in the 45-degree straight line on the upper side of the diagonally drawn straight line. This means that many firms have increased the number of firms for sales.

The number of transaction firms (All: Figure 3) is also similar to that in Figures 1-2; that is, when the number of transition firms is high, the number tends to increase, because there seems to be many firms

Chapter 6 Dynamics of the Network Structure and Activity of Japanese Firms 87

In-degree (the number of purchasing firms)

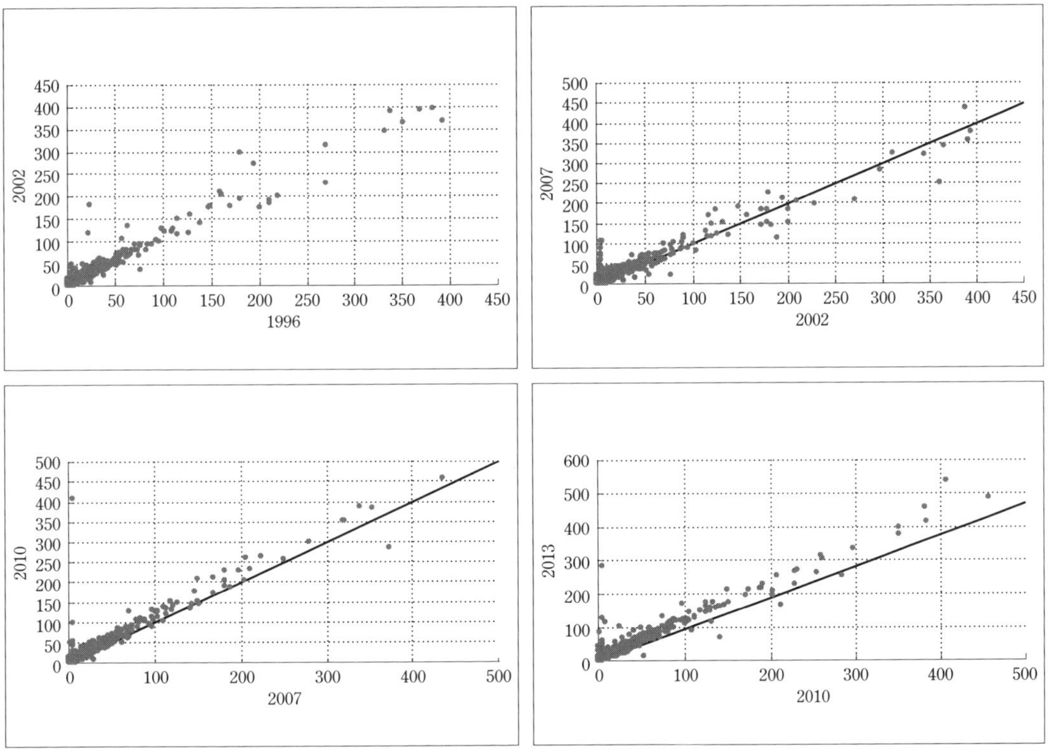

Figure 1 : Plot of Correlation of the In-Degree

Out-degree (the number of Selling firms)

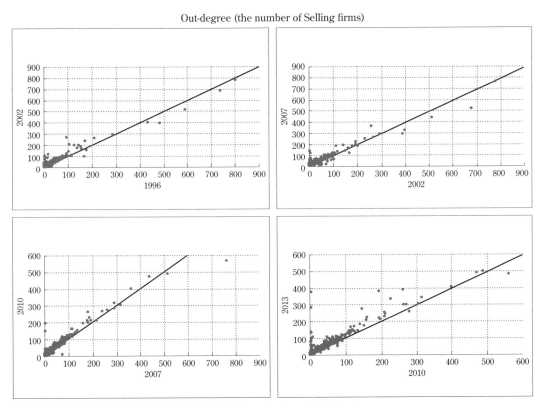

Figure 2 : Plot of Correlation of the Out-Degree

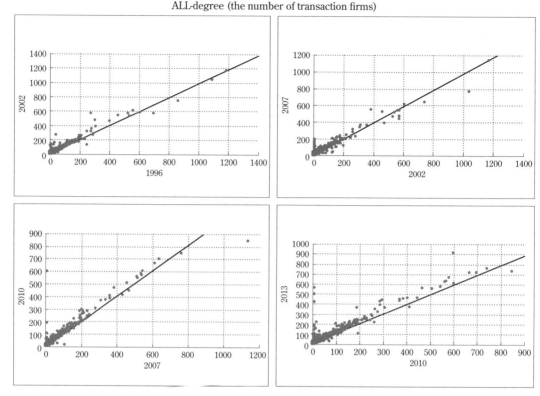

Figure 3 : Plot of Correlation of the ALL-Degree

in the 45-degree straight line on the upper side of the diagonally drawn straight line. However, in 2002-2007, the rate of decreasing transaction firms seems to decrease.

Next, when we see the transition of closeness, it does not seem that the tendency of increasing it exists. In Figures 4-6 many firms are on the horizontal (or vertical) axis; this was the reason why some firms reported 0 for the purchasing or sales firms.

The result of betweenness is similar to the degree (Figure 7). That is, higher number of betweenness leads it to increase in the next year. There are many firms where the diagonally drawn straight line exceeds the 45-degree straight line, and the large betweenness firm intends to increase it.

5. Conclusion

In this study, we estimate some indexes of network centrality for each firm during 1996-2013 and examine their changes. The number of purchasing or selling firms is 6-8 on average, and the median is 5. The average is larger than the median, the histogram is left-skewed, and few firms take large degrees, as in previous literature.

To analyze the relationship between firm size (sales or employee) and network centrality (degree, closeness, and betweenness), degree and betweenness are highly correlated to firm size. On the contrary, closeness is not correlated to firm size. This means that in the transition relationship, large firms do not take

Closeness (the purchasing firms)

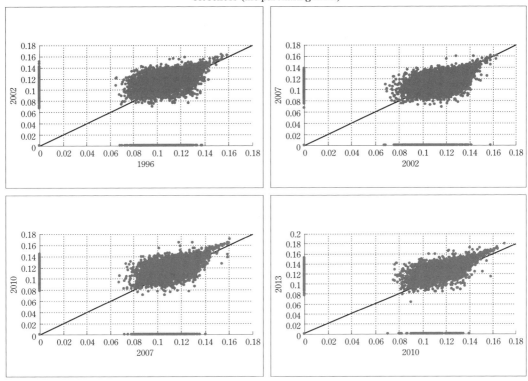

Figure 4 : Correlation of Closeness (In-Degree)

Closeness (the selling firms)

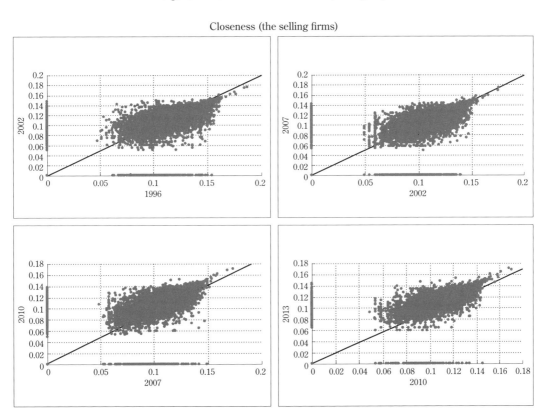

Figure 5 : The correlation of Closeness (Out-Degree)

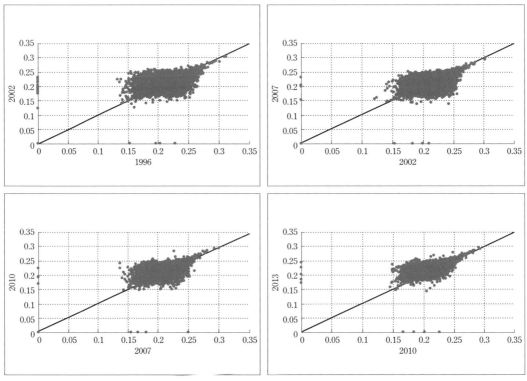

Figure 6 : Correlation of Closeness (ALL-Degree)

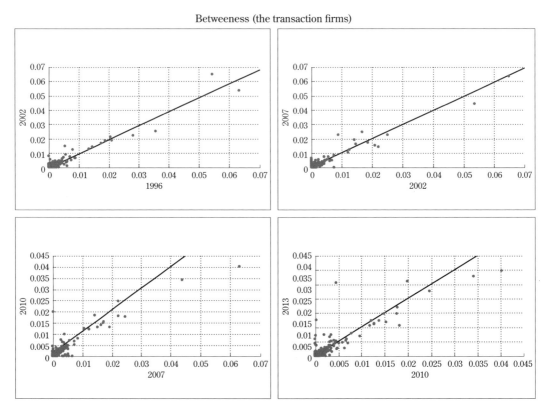

Figure 7 : Correlation of Betweenness (ALL-Degree)

a position of closer distance in the network.

For the transition of each firm's centrality in the time series, firms with high degree or betweenness will continue the condition after several years. It is observed that the degree or betweenness is increased in continuous firms, and "Matthew's law" exists in the network theory.

However, this result is only applicable for firms operating continuously during 1996-2013. Other firms (not continuous or entry firms) are not included in our analysis. It is necessary to conduct similar analyses for them.

References

Goto, H., H. Takayasu, and M. Takayasu (2015), "Empirical Analysis of Firm-Dynamics on Japanese Inter-firm Trade Network," In Proceedings of the International Conference on Social Modeling and Simulation, Plus Econophysics Colloquium 2014.

Hisa. Y., S. Hisa, and H. Okuda (2016), "Network Centrality of Transaction on Firms and FDI and Withdraw," *Research of Economics and Trade* (Kanagawa University), 42, pp.33-43.

Masuda N., and N. Konno (2010), *Complex Networks, from the Basics to the Advance, Fukuzatsu Network Kiso kara Ouyou made,* Kindai Kagaku Sha (in Japanese).

Ohnishi, T., H. Takayasu, and T. Takayasu (2010), "The Mathematical Principle Structure of the Transaction of Firms," *Application Mathematics,* 20(3), pp.37-49.

Takayasu, M., S. Sameshima, T. Ohnishi, Y. Ikeda, H. Takayasu, and K. Watanabe (2007), "Massive Economics Data Analysis by Econophysics Methods: The Case of Companies' Network Structure," *Annual Report of the Earth Simulator Center,* p.263-267.

Chapter 7

Comparison of the Potential Competitiveness of Asian Countries

Nariyasu YAMASAWA

Abstract

A country's competitiveness is an important factor for both companies and governments that focus on country rankings published by institutes such as the Institute for Management Development (IMD) and World Economic Forum (WEF). However, the definition of competitiveness varies by publication. We define competitiveness from an economic point of view as the increase of per-capita gross domestic product and potential competitiveness in a ten-year forecast. We develop a ranking system based on the potential competitiveness of Asian countries, including ASEAN countries, China, India, Hong Kong, Korea, and Japan. We selected these countries because Southeast Asia is the most rapidly developing region in the world and it is useful to understand its current economic status. To compile the potential competitiveness index, we use various economic and social indicators, such as (1) education expenditure (% of GNI), (2) mobile cellular subscriptions (per 100 people), (3) life expectancy at birth, total (years), and (4) urban population (% of total). Our selection of indicators for an item such as education or science and technology varies with the characteristics of the item, but is founded in endogenous growth theory. Each indicator reveals the factors that contribute to a country's competitiveness. We develop potential competitiveness based on an analysis of data from a 2016 data set. Our ranking places Hong Kong and Singapore in the first and second places in terms of potential competitiveness, respectively.

JEL: O47

Keywords: Competitiveness, Asian Economies, Economic Growth, Aggregate Productivity

1. Introduction

A country's competitiveness is an important notion for companies and governments. The Japanese government set up an industrial competitiveness council in 2013, which was later succeeded by the Future Investment Council. While businesses and governments focus on a country's competitiveness rankings, the definition of competitiveness varies by publication.

The World Competitiveness Report (WCR) by the Institute for Management Development (IMD) and the World Economic Forum (WEF) is a study that rates and ranks the competitiveness of a certain group of countries and is widely quoted in international media.

The IMD and WEF publish competitiveness rankings every year. However, their detailed methods are not revealed, and their definition of competitiveness remains nebulous.

We thus follow the Japan Center for Economic Research (JCER 2011) for the definition of competitiveness. They define competitiveness from an economic point of view. According to JCER, potential competitiveness is not an outcome of economic growth, but the ability to be competitive in the future. With our survey, we seek primarily to determine if a country is equipped with the necessary foundation to improve competitiveness in the future. For example, high rates of education and good infrastructure indicate strong potential competitiveness.

We update the data and expand the number of Asian countries to ascertain the competitiveness of Cambodia, Lao, Myanmar, and Vietnam (CLMV). Southeast Asia is the most rapidly developing region in the world; and it is necessary, for both academic and business purposes, to critically understand this region.

2. Literature Review

The IMD (2017) World Competitiveness Rankings and the WEF (2016) The Global Competitiveness Report are popular global rankings. Oral and Chabchoub (1996) attempted to uncover the methodology of the WCR using mathematical programming. Petrarca and Terzi (2018) presented the alternative method of the Global Competitiveness Index (GCI) by means of a partial least squares path model. They successfully uncover the competitiveness ranking mathematical method, but their discussion is not based on economic theory such as endogenous growth theory.

There are many concepts of competitiveness. Brunner and Calí (2006) and Erber et al. (1997) focused on industrial competitiveness with an emphasis on trade and industrial policy. Williamson et al. (2018) developed an alternative benchmark for China's growth on an industry-by-industry basis.

Institutional competitiveness is a broader concept. Huang (2007) discussed institutional competitiveness and institutional aging. Yamasawa (2013) discussed the middle-income trap from the viewpoint of institutional competitiveness. Demographic factors also affect competitiveness. Cai (2012) discussed the influence of the demographic factor on China's growth.

Our definition of competitiveness follows JCER (2011), which clarifies the data selection methodology and asserts data selection based on the endogenous growth theory originally presented by Hall and Jones (1999).

3. Measures of Competitiveness

3. 1. Survey of Competitiveness

We survey measures of competitiveness in this study. Competitiveness has many definitions. For example, high-level education or labor productivity can be an indicator of the competitiveness of a nation, and also a "cause" of its competitiveness. Further, an increase in income is an indicator and "result" of a nation's competitiveness.

3. 2. IMD : World Competitiveness Yearbook

The IMD, based in Switzerland, began publishing its set of representative competitiveness indicators in The World Competitiveness Yearbook in 1990. The IMD ranks competitiveness using a variety of indicators. It uses not only hard data, such as gross domestic product (GDP), but also soft data, such as questionnaire surveys.

In 1990, the report ranked Japan in first place, a position it occupied until the United States of America took over in 1995. In the 2010s, Singapore and Hong Kong moved into the first place. Japan experienced a very rapid decline in its competitiveness ranking, falling to thirtieth place in 2002. Though Japan's ranking rose in 2003, it continued to decline thereafter.

3. 3. WEF : The Global Competitiveness Report

The Global Competitiveness Report (GCR) by the WEF is another popular competitiveness ranking. The GCR is published every year; in 2016-2017, it investigated the competitiveness of 138 countries and regions. It defines competitiveness as a combination of institutions, policies and the economy, prioritizing productivity for the economic factor. The GCI combines 114 indicators that capture concepts affecting productivity and long-term prosperity. In this report, Japan ranked relatively high at ninth place in 2017, while the IMD ranked it twenty-sixth.

3. 4. GDP Growth Rate

The GDP growth rate is important with respect to competitiveness. However, growth rates tend to be high for developing countries. From 2010-2016, China and Lao PDR recorded the highest growth rate among the 13 countries and economies listed in Table 1 at 7.7%. Further, Myanmar, India, Bangladesh, Philippines, Vietnam, and Cambodia exhibit base growth rates of over 6%. Developed economies tend to show lower growth rates than their developing counterparts.

3. 5. Per-capita GNI

The International Monetary Fund uses per-capita GNI (Gross National Income) to classify countries as high-income (over 12,235 USD) and low-income (below 1,005 USD). Figure 1 shows these classifications. This metric is useful in assessing a country's current conditions, but it cannot forecast future conditions because it is a static indicator.

3. 6. Increase in Per-capita GDP

The level of per-capita GDP may be an indicator of a country's competitiveness but the per-capita increase in GDP is a more relevant indicator. As a measurement of growth, we can regard the rate of change as an indicator of competitiveness, in which case, the lower the level of GDP, the higher the rate of growth will be in general. A highly competitive country in the present should naturally be considered more competitive than a country without existing competitiveness. It is thus not appropriate to use the rate of change in the calculation of competitiveness. We therefore consider the amount of change in

Chapter 7 Comparison of the Potential Competitiveness of Asian Countries   95

Table 1 : Real Growth Rates of Asian Countries and Economies(Annual Rate / %)

Country Name	1980-1990	1990-2000	2000-2010	2010-2016
China	9.3	10.4	10.6	7.7
Lao PDR		6.2	7.1	7.7
Cambodia			7.9	7.1
Myanmar	1.3	7.2	12.0	7.0
India	5.6	5.6	7.5	6.9
Bangladesh	4.0	4.7	5.6	6.5
Philippines	1.7	2.9	4.8	6.1
Vietnam		7.6	6.6	6.0
Sri Lanka	4.2	5.2	5.2	5.9
Indonesia	5.5	3.9	5.2	5.4
Malaysia	6.0	7.1	4.6	5.1
Pakistan	6.3	3.9	4.2	4.3
Singapore	7.7	7.1	5.8	4.0
Thailand	7.8	4.4	4.6	3.0
Korea, Rep.	9.9	6.9	4.4	3.0
Hong Kong SAR, China	6.7	4.0	4.1	2.8
Japan	4.5	1.3	0.6	1.0

Source : *World Development Indicators,* The World Bank.

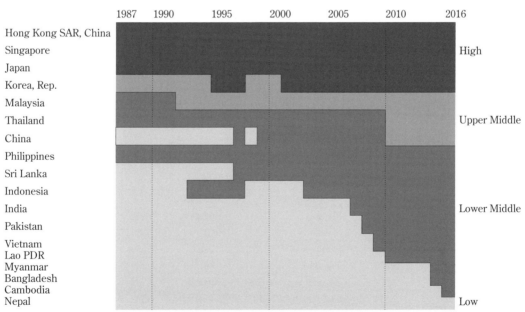

In 2016, Low income (L) <= 1,005, Lower middle income (LM) 1,006-3,955, Upper middle income (UM) 3,956-12,235, High income (H) > 12,235
Note : Classified by GNI per capita in USD (Atlas methodology).

Figure 1 : The World Bank Analytical Classifications

per-capita GDP as a competitiveness indicator that adds the level of GDP to the rate of change as follows:

$$\text{Level} \times \text{rate of change} = \text{amount of change}$$

3. 7. JCER : Potential Competitiveness Report

JCER published the "Potential Competitiveness Report" from 2004 to 2010, using increase in per-capita GDP as an overall competitiveness indicator. While the IMD uses questionnaire surveys, the JCER report features quantitative analyses based on available socio-economic data.

We adopt the methodology of JCER (2011). Its advantage is the clearness of the definition of competitiveness by GDP statistics. Since GDP statistics are available for almost all countries, the data are easily obtained and the transparency of the methodology ensured.

The methodology indicates the outcomes of high competitiveness, and can be estimated without survey data, which may be prone to subjective bias.

4. Methodology

4. 1. Per-Capita GDP Ranking

JCER (2011) defines the increase in per-capita GDP as a country's competitiveness. Table 2 provides a ranking of 50 countries according to the increase in per-capita GDP. This ranking provides a meaningful indication of each country's competitiveness at specific points in time. Japan, Norway, and Singapore ranked first in the 1980s, 1990s, and 2000s, respectively. Ireland moved to first place in the 2010s after exceptionally high growth in 2015 following the relocation of the headquarters of a number of firms to Ireland. Among Asian economies, the highest-ranking countries in the 2010s were Singapore, Hong Kong, and Korea.

Table 2 : Per-Capita GDP Ranking

	1980-1990		1990-2000		2000-2010		2010-2016	
1	Japan	12,417	Norway	21,447	Singapore	13,180	Ireland	18,249
2	Norway	11,734	Ireland	19,876	Hong Kong	9,534	Singapore	6,031
3	Switzerland	9,384	Denmark	11,282	Australia	7,650	Sweden	4,243
4	Singapore	8,869	Singapore	11,212	Sweden	7,383	Hong Kong	4,176
5	Denmark	8,191	Netherlands	10,650	Switzerland	6,991	United States	3,821
6	Finland	7,854	United States	8,743	Korea, Rep.	6,982	Australia	3,797
7	United States	7,578	Australia	8,396	Norway	5,914	Germany	3,766
8	Hong Kong	7,524	Austria	8,155	Finland	5,752	Turkey	3,399
9	United Kingdom	6,833	Sweden	7,181	Ireland	5,152	Korea, Rep.	3,372
10	Ireland	6,550	Canada	7,149	Czech	4,997	New Zealand	3,151

Note : Increase in per-capita GDP (constant 2010 USD).

Chapter 7   Comparison of the Potential Competitiveness of Asian Countries   97

4. 2. Potential Competitiveness

JCER (2011) estimates potential competitiveness, which refers to the current potential of a country to compete over the next ten years. For example, the potential competitiveness indicator as of 1980 shows a country's ability to increase its per-capita GDP over the 1980s. In other words, potential competitiveness is a forecast of competitiveness at the initial point.

Potential competitiveness and realized competitiveness do not correspond completely. Unforeseen events can occur over the next ten years, and we acknowledge this uncertainty.

To compile our rankings, we use the per-capita increase in GDP to judge international competitiveness, and then look for the factors that increase the per-capita increase in GDP for each item.

1. Define per-capita increase of GDP as international competitiveness
2. Select variables that are likely to be associated with per-capita GDP increase in the future; data selection is founded in endogenous growth theory
3. Use a regression to ensure that the variable is appropriate
4. Compile the variables using a principal component analysis, where the first principal component should represent competitiveness
5. Estimate the potential competitive index
6. Determine the potential competitiveness ranking

4. 3. Model

To ensure that we select the appropriate variables, we tested the coefficients of the following equation, where GDP_{it} is GDP, POP_{it} is population, α and β are parameters, and x_{it} is the first principal component of the potential competitiveness factors:

$$\Delta\left(\frac{GDP_{it}}{POP_{it}}\right)=\alpha+\beta x_{it-1}+\varepsilon_{it}$$

We use panel data with cross sectional data comprising ASEAN countries, South Asian countries, China, Hong Kong, Korea, and Japan. We use time series data for 1980, 1990, and 2000. We estimate with both fixed and random effects models.

The equation is an appropriate measure of potential competitiveness. x_{it} is the initial point of GDP increase over ten years. Series x_{it} in 1980 will influence the increase in per-capita GDP from 1980 to 1990, and so on. The potential competitiveness in the latest period will influence competitiveness over the next ten years. Since the competitiveness variables may be correlated, there may be a multicollinearity problem. We therefore compile the 13 variables using principal component analysis.

4. 4. Analysis of Regional Effects

In the first analysis, we investigate spatial effect by estimating a spatial model. We use a weighted matrix w_{ij}, designed such that countries that share a border have mutual economic effects (Anselin 1988).

$$\Delta\left(\frac{GDP_{it}}{POP_{it}}\right)=\rho\sum_{j=1}^{n}w_{ij}\Delta\left(\frac{GDP_{jt}}{POP_{jt}}\right)+\beta x_{it-1}+\varepsilon_{it}$$

If ρ is significant, then a spatial effect exists.

In the second analysis, we use dummy variables for country groups. The country groups are ASEAN, ASEAN4 (Indonesia, Malaysia, Philippines and Thailand), CLMV, and South Asia (India, Bangladesh, Pakistan, and Sri Lanka). If the country i belongs to the country group, D_i is 1. If the country i doesn't belong to the country group, D_i is zero. If coefficient γ is significant, a region-specific effect exists in terms of the possibility that a potential competitiveness factor will increase per-capita GDP. That is,

$$\Delta\left(\frac{GDP_{it}}{POP_{it}}\right)=\alpha+\beta x_{it-1}+\gamma D_i x_{it-1}+\varepsilon_{it}$$

5. Data

5. 1. Variation in GDP Statistics

We define the increase in per-capita GDP as a competitiveness indicator. However, there are many kinds of GDP-related statistics. Researchers use both GDP and GNI to discuss the middle-income trap (Yamasawa 2013). If we focus on multinational companies, GNI is appropriate, but it will be difficult to distinguish between the competitiveness of countries and the competitiveness of companies. Thus, GDP is an appropriate measure of a country's competitiveness.

GDP can be measured in terms of nominal or current prices and real or constant prices. Since the nominal value fluctuates with domestic prices, a constant price GDP is appropriate. The current USD-based GDP is influenced by not only domestic prices, but also the exchange rate. Purchasing power parity (PPP)-based GDP has the additional influence of domestic/foreign price differences.

International comparison requires a unified unit, which may be dollar-based or PPP-based. We adopt the USD as a measure that is exchangeable via trade. A PPP-based measurement indicates the strength of a country's domestic purchasing power, but for international comparison, a measurement based on the internationally arbitrated USD value is more appropriate.

Note that for the constant price basis, the growth rates are the same for the PPP-based, USD-based, and local currency-based GDP. We conclude that the increase in per-capita GDP measured by using constant USD values is the best way to rank competitiveness.

5. 2. Variable Selection

We try to compile a potential competitiveness ranking for ASEAN4, CLMV, and South Asia. However, there is a constraint in data availability for estimating competitiveness. JCER uses 30 indicators to compile potential competitiveness, but gathering this data is impossible without creating new data for CLMV and South Asia. We therefore select variables in view of both correlation and availability. We use the

Chapter 7　Comparison of the Potential Competitiveness of Asian Countries　99

Table 3 : Variable Selection

Series Name	Correlation Coeffficient				No. of samples	Available Sample Rate	Index
	1980	1990	2000 ①	average	②	③=②/651	①×③
1　Population density (people per sq. km of land area)	0.2	0.6	0.5	0.4	616	0.95	0.49
2　Population ages 40-44, female (% of female population)	0.4	0.4	0.5	0.4	580	0.89	0.44
3　Concessional debt (% of total external debt)	0.1	0.0	−0.6	0.2	376	0.58	0.35
4　Fixed telephone subscriptions (per 100 people)	0.4	0.2	0.4	0.3	567	0.87	0.34
5　Mobile cellular subscriptions (per 100 people)	0.1	0.2	0.3	0.2	611	0.94	0.32
6　Rural population growth (annual %)	−0.5	−0.4	−0.3	0.4	627	0.96	0.29
7　Life expectancy at birth, total (years)	0.3	0.5	0.3	0.3	589	0.90	0.28
8　Age dependency ratio (% of working-age population)	−0.2	−0.1	−0.3	0.2	502	0.77	0.26
9　Survival to age 65, male (% of cohort)	0.2	0.5	0.3	0.3	582	0.89	0.25
10　Physicians (per 1,000 people)	0.2	0.2	0.5	0.3	338	0.52	0.25
11　Machinery and transport equipment (% of value added in manufacturing)	0.7	0.1	0.4	0.4	366	0.56	0.24
12　Gross fixed capital formation, private sector (% of GDP)	0.2	0.2	0.5	0.3	291	0.45	0.24
13　School enrollment, secondary (% gross)	0.3	0.2	0.4	0.3	374	0.57	0.22
14　Mortality rate, infant (per 1,000 live births)	−0.3	−0.5	−0.3	0.3	557	0.86	0.22

Note : "Correlation coefficient 1980" means correlation between series in 1980 and per-capita △GDP 1980-1990. The full sample of 651 is the number of all countries (217) multiplied by three terms.

world development indicators of the World Bank, which contain 1,574 series. We then check the correlation between the variables in 1980, 1990, and 2000, and the per-capita △GDP in 1980-1990, 1990-2000, and 2000-2010, respectively, for all 271 countries. We also calculate the data availability rate as the ratio of available data to all possible data. If all data are available, the figure will be 651 (217×3), where there are 217 countries and three periods.

We build the index by multiplying the correlation coefficient by the availability rate (Table 3). This index shows the degree of both correlation and availability for the variables. Sorting by this index, we choose 14 series. However, given the lack of data for machinery and transport equipment in 2016, we use 13 series.

Machinery and transport equipment data are sufficient for the estimate, but to calculate the potential competitiveness, we need the latest data.

5. 3. Classification

To analyze the results, we classify the 13 series into seven categories (Table 4). Table 5 shows descriptive statistics of potential competitiveness factors. The demography category includes the female population aged 40-44 years and the age dependency ratio. The lifespan category includes male survivors up to the age of 65 years, life expectancy at birth, and the infant mortality rate. The debt category includes concessional debt, which is defined as loans with an original grant element of 25% or more. The telecommunication category includes fixed telephone and mobile cellular subscriptions. The agglomeration category includes population density and rural population growth. The science and education category includes the number of physicians and secondary school enrollments.

6. Estimation Result

Table 6 reports the estimation result. According to the table, the Hausman test does not reject the hypothesis that a random effect is correct. We thus use the result of the random effect.

Table 4 : Potential Competitiveness Factors by Categories

	Demography		Telecommunication
	Population ages 40-44, female		Fixed telephone subscriptions
(−)	Age dependency ratio		Mobile cellular subscriptions
	Lifespan		Agglomeration
	Survival to age 65, male		Population density
	Life expectancy at birth, total	(−)	Rural population growth
(−)	Mortality rate, infant		Science and Education
	Debt		Physicians
(−)	Concessional debt		School enrollment, secondary
	Investment		
	Gross fixed capital formation, private sector (% of GDP)		

Table 5 : Descriptive Statistics of Potential Competitiveness Factors

	Population density (people per sq. km of land area)	Population ages 40-44, female (% of female population)	Concessional debt (% of total external debt)	Fixed telephone subscriptions (per 100 people)	Mobile cellular subscriptions (per 100 people)	Rural population growth (annual %)	Life expectancy at birth, total (years)	Age dependency ratio (% of working-age population)	Survival to age 65, male (% of cohort)	Physicians (per 1,000 people)	Gross fixed capital formation, private sector (% of GDP)	School enrollment, secondary (% gross)	Mortality rate, infant (per 1,000 live births)
Mean	925.5	6.0	32.6	13.5	45.9	−0.5	68.7	59.4	67.0	0.8	17.8	62.3	39.8
Median	221.3	5.8	20.8	3.2	2.3	0.4	69.1	57.9	66.2	0.5	17.9	63.3	29.7
Maximum	7,908.7	9.8	99.2	62.1	240.8	2.8	84.2	92.0	89.6	3.6	35.0	120.6	135.5
Minimum	14.1	3.7	0.0	0.0	0.0	−62.6	27.5	33.2	19.9	0.1	3.2	17.0	2.0
Std. Dev.	1,931.9	1.5	33.0	18.7	58.6	7.1	9.2	16.8	12.8	0.7	7.1	27.6	36.0
Observations	85	85	85	85	85	85	85	85	85	85	85	85	85
Cross sections	17	17	17	17	17	17	17	17	17	17	17	17	17

Table 6 : Estimation Result

Dependent Variable: Δ GDP per capita
Total pool (unbalanced) observations: 47

Variable	Fixed Coefficient	Random Coefficient
C	2,174.15 ***	2,265.88 ***
PCA	1,187.41 *	1,015.55 ***
Adjusted R-squared	0.795	0.541
Houseman Test(P-Value) (random effect is correct)	0.7755	

Note : Δ GDP1: increase in per-capita GDP (constant 2010 USD), C: constant coefficient, PCA: First principal component of 13 valuables. * p＜0.1, *** p＜0.01.

6. 1. Potential Competitiveness Ranking

We create a potential competitiveness ranking as the estimate or forecast in the increase in per-capita GDP according to the first component of 13 series (Table 7).

The latest ranking means that high-ranking countries and economies will have greater competitiveness in the future because current conditions affect future per-capita GDP. This ranking lists Hong Kong in first place and Singapore in second. The CLMV and South Asian countries show low competitiveness. While the growth rate is high, it takes time to increase per-capita GDP. Vietnam and Sri Lanka have relatively high potential competitiveness in 2016. Vietnam is in eighth place and Sri Lanka in tenth. Myanmar and Pakistan show low potential competitiveness. Myanmar is in fifteenth place and Pakistan is in the lowest position, that is, seventeenth place.

We checked the difference between rankings from 2010 to 2016. The ranking of potential competitiveness in 2010 and 2016 is the same for the countries from first to eighth place. Among the CLMV and South Asian countries, Lao PDR's rank rose from fifteenth to thirteenth place. Bangladesh's rank rose from twelfth to eleventh place, and Myanmar's rose from sixteenth to fifteenth place.

We can check the factors of potential competitiveness. Table 8 shows deviation values for countries. Appendix 1 provides more detail from the tables. Deviation values of CLMV and South Asian countries are below 50, indicating that these categories are lower than the average for most Asian countries. If the deviation value is less than 40, the factors are weak points of these countries. For Lao PDR, the values of lifespan and demography are under 40. There are four factors under 40 for Cambodia, and three factors under 40 for Myanmar. Vietnam has no categories under 40.

For South Asian Countries, India has no category under 40. Pakistan has five categories under 40, while Bangladesh has one category under 40.

6. 2. Empirical Result of Regional Effect

We examine the regional effect using the weighted matrix analysis. However, the estimation result shows that a special effect does not exist (Table 9). Even if two countries have a common border, it does not mean the two countries influence each other.

Then we examine the regional effect using the dummy variables (Table 10). In the first estimation, we

Table 7 : Potential Competitiveness Ranking

Potential Competitiveness Index (constant 2010 US$)

Country	1980	Country	1990	Country	2000	Country	2010	Country	2016
Singapore	9,174	Singapore	9,745	Singapore	9,820	Singapore	8,919	Singapore	8,746
Japan	7,033	Hong Kong	7,864	Hong Kong	7,312	Hong Kong	6,921	Hong Kong	6,837
Hong Kong	6,376	Japan	6,566	Korea, Rep.	6,714	Korea, Rep.	6,432	Korea, Rep.	5,976
Korea, Rep.	4,884	Korea, Rep.	5,535	Japan	5,722	Japan	5,106	Japan	4,702
China	2,207	Malaysia	2,311	Malaysia	2,479	China	3,395	China	3,319
Malaysia	2,167	Thailand	2,066	China	2,332	Thailand	2,351	Thailand	2,857
Sri Lanka	1,520	China	1,544	Thailand	1,725	Malaysia	2,181	Malaysia	2,067
Thailand	1,180	Sri Lanka	1,024	Vietnam	1,472	Vietnam	2,036	Vietnam	1,908
Philippines	1,102	Indonesia	915	Sri Lanka	1,224	Sri Lanka	1,082	Indonesia	1,192
Vietnam	1,053	Philippines	588	Indonesia	920	Indonesia	1,035	Sri Lanka	833
Indonesia	677	India	419	India	292	India	418	Bangladesh	728
India	486	Vietnam	278	Bangladesh	231	Bangladesh	314	India	421
Pakistan	335	Pakistan	195	Philippines	189	Philippines	15	Lao PDR	403
Myanmar	287	Cambodia	−9	Myanmar	130	Cambodia	−75	Cambodia	164
Bangladesh	107	Myanmar	−74	Pakistan	−495	Lao PDR	−124	Myanmar	24
Cambodia	95	Bangladesh	−181	Lao PDR	−610	Myanmar	−467	Philippines	−299
Lao PDR	−163	Lao PDR	−266	Cambodia	−937	Pakistan	−1,021	Pakistan	−1,358

Table 8 : Deviation Value in 2016

Deviation 2016

	Lao PDR	Vietnam	Cambodia	Myanmar	India	Pakistan	Bangladesh	Sri Lanka
Demography	38.2	54.4	38.2	49.9	46.0	33.6	46.1	47.6
Lifespan	37.2	51.3	43.6	38.2	41.6	35.1	47.2	52.5
Debt	42.3	43.1	37.1	30.1	55.2	39.9	33.4	46.1
Investment	52.3	45.1	37.6	63.0	49.3	29.5	56.1	53.2
Telecommunication	42.8	47.8	46.5	42.7	41.7	39.9	41.1	48.9
Agglomeration	47.3	46.9	43.3	46.4	45.9	43.8	49.3	44.4
Science and Education	41.6	55.0	34.9	40.6	45.0	39.5	42.0	50.8

Table 9 : Estimation Result

Dependent Variable: Per-capita ΔGDP
Total pool (unbalanced) observations: 47

Variable	Random Coefficient
C	2,157.22 ***
PCA	1,001.56 ***
WΔGDP per capita	0.12
Adjusted R-squared	0.518
Houseman Test(P-Value) (random effect is correct)	0.4772

Note : *** p<0.01.

Table 10 : Estimation Result

Dependent Variable: Per-capita △GDP
Total pool (unbalanced) observations: 47

Variable	Random Coefficient	Random Coefficient
C	2,166.21 ***	2,174.15 **
PCA	1,029.34 ***	1,187.41 ***
PCA*ASEAN	55.77	
PCA*ASEAN4		−688.56
PCA*CLMV		−1,126.15 ***
PCA*SOUTH	−279.77	−1,024.90 ***
PCA*SGP		896.11 ***
Adjusted R-squared	0.518	0.841
Houseman Test (P-Value) (random effect is correct)	0.7803	0.8407

Note : ** p<0.05, *** p<0.01.

use dummy variables for ASEAN and Southeast Asia. The baseline is East Asia. The results show no significant country group effect. However, if we divide ASEAN countries into ASEAN4, CLMV, and Singapore, the group effects of Southeast, CLMV, and Singapore are significant. This evidences a country group effect. The group effects for CLMV and South Asia are significantly negative, while that for Singapore is significantly positive.

7. Discussion

As noted earlier, our methodology is based on JCER's methodology, although we extend our target countries to CLMV and South Asia. This is the first time the competitiveness of all these countries has been quantified. Additionally, we also measured the factors that influence competitiveness and potential competitiveness. This helps us identify the strengths and weaknesses of these countries.

JCER (2011) does not consider CLMV and South Asian countries, except Vietnam, India, and Pakistan. CLMV and South Asian countries are rapidly developing regions in the world and it is useful to understand their economic status. We consider these countries and reveal their competitiveness. While JCER's data dates to 2009, we use updated data from 2016.

Nevertheless, this study's limitation is the scarcity of data. We expect the data of CLMV and South Asian countries to be updated further. Once such optimum data are available, we expect newer studies to recalculate competitiveness.

8. Conclusion

We define competitiveness as an increase in per-capita GDP and estimate the potential competitiveness for a group of Asian countries. We select variables related to an increase in per-capita GDP over the next ten years. We also consider data availability and select 13 series, which we divide into categories such as demography, lifespan, and so on. We also estimate potential competitiveness indicators that show future competitiveness. According to the latest data, Singapore, Hong Kong, and Korea rank in first, second, and third places in the potential competitiveness ranking.

For CLMV and South Asia, Vietnam, and Sri Lanka had relatively high potential competitiveness in 2016, while Myanmar and Pakistan showed low potential competitiveness for the same year.

Appendix

Table 11 : Rank of Competitiveness-Related Indicators

Population density (people per sq. km of land area)

Country	1980	Country	1990	Country	2000	Country	2010	Country	2016
HKG	5,063.1	HKG	5,762.1	HKG	6,347.6	SGP	7,231.8	SGP	7,908.7
SGP	3,602.9	SGP	4,548.0	SGP	6,011.8	HKG	6,689.7	HKG	6,987.2
BGD	625.9	BGD	815.8	BGD	1,010.8	BGD	1,168.8	BGD	1,251.8
KOR	395.2	KOR	444.4	KOR	487.3	KOR	509.7	KOR	525.7
JPN	318.8	JPN	338.8	IND	354.2	IND	414.0	IND	445.4
LKA	239.8	IND	292.7	JPN	348.0	JPN	351.3	JPN	348.4
IND	234.4	LKA	276.3	LKA	299.5	LKA	322.1	PHL	346.5
VNM	167.0	VNM	209.6	PHL	261.6	PHL	314.3	LKA	338.1
PHL	159.0	PHL	207.8	VNM	258.1	VNM	285.3	VNM	305.0
CHN	104.5	PAK	139.7	PAK	179.7	PAK	221.3	PAK	250.6
PAK	101.3	CHN	120.9	CHN	134.5	CHN	142.5	CHN	146.9
THA	92.8	THA	110.8	THA	123.2	IDN	133.9	IDN	144.1
IDN	81.4	IDN	100.2	IDN	116.8	THA	131.6	THA	134.8
MMR	51.1	MMR	62.2	MYS	70.6	MYS	85.6	MYS	94.9
MYS	42.0	MYS	54.9	MMR	70.5	KHM	81.1	KHM	89.3
KHM	37.9	KHM	50.8	KHM	68.8	MMR	76.8	MMR	81.0
LAO	14.1	LAO	18.5	LAO	23.1	LAO	27.1	LAO	29.3

Population ages 40-44, female (% of female population)

Country	1980	Country	1990	Country	2000	Country	2010	Country	2016
JPN	7.0	JPN	8.4	HKG	9.8	CHN	9.4	HKG	8.5
SGP	5.5	SGP	7.3	SGP	9.5	HKG	8.9	THA	8.3
KOR	5.5	HKG	6.5	KOR	8.5	THA	8.8	SGP	8.3
IDN	5.0	KOR	5.7	THA	8.0	KOR	8.7	CHN	8.2
IND	5.0	LKA	5.7	LKA	7.0	SGP	8.2	KOR	8.1
THA	4.9	THA	5.6	CHN	6.6	IDN	6.9	JPN	7.5
LKA	4.8	CHN	5.4	MYS	6.3	VNM	6.8	VNM	7.1
HKG	4.8	MYS	5.2	VNM	6.2	LKA	6.6	IDN	7.1
MYS	4.7	IND	4.8	JPN	6.0	JPN	6.6	MMR	6.8
BGD	4.7	IDN	4.5	MMR	5.9	MMR	6.5	LKA	6.6
CHN	4.6	MMR	4.3	IDN	5.9	MYS	6.3	BGD	6.3
PAK	4.5	PHL	4.2	IND	5.6	BGD	6.2	IND	6.3
KHM	4.3	KHM	4.2	PHL	5.4	IND	5.9	MYS	6.2
LAO	4.2	BGD	4.2	KHM	5.0	PHL	5.9	PHL	5.8
MMR	4.1	PAK	4.2	PAK	4.6	KHM	5.6	LAO	5.5
PHL	4.0	LAO	3.9	BGD	4.5	PAK	5.1	PAK	5.2
VNM	4.0	VNM	3.7	LAO	4.2	LAO	4.9	KHM	5.0

Chapter 7　Comparison of the Potential Competitiveness of Asian Countries　105

Concessional debt (% of total external debt)

Country	1980	Country	1990	Country	2000	Country	2010	Country	2016
VNM	0.0	HKG	0.0	HKG	0.0	HKG	0.0	HKG	0.0
KHM	0.0	KOR	0.0	KOR	0.0	KOR	0.0	KOR	0.0
HKG	0.0	JPN	0.0	JPN	0.0	JPN	0.0	JPN	0.0
CHN	0.0	SGP	0.0	SGP	0.0	SGP	0.0	SGP	0.0
KOR	0.0	MYS	14.6	MYS	7.0	MYS	2.6	MYS	0.7
JPN	0.0	THA	15.2	THA	11.5	CHN	5.4	CHN	1.4
SGP	0.0	CHN	17.6	CHN	20.8	THA	6.3	THA	3.4
PHL	5.5	PHL	20.0	IDN	21.2	IND	17.5	IDN	8.2
MYS	8.6	IDN	26.4	PHL	21.4	IDN	23.1	IND	10.1
THA	10.0	KHM	44.8	IND	38.1	PHL	24.0	PHL	10.8
IDN	36.4	IND	48.0	PAK	54.7	PAK	53.8	LKA	32.7
LKA	56.2	PAK	58.5	VNM	62.0	VNM	55.5	VNM	40.3
PAK	71.6	LKA	71.9	MMR	71.4	LAO	55.9	LAO	42.1
MMR	73.4	VNM	85.2	LKA	73.4	LKA	57.2	PAK	48.1
IND	75.7	MMR	88.1	KHM	94.7	MMR	71.7	KHM	55.2
BGD	79.8	BGD	90.6	BGD	94.8	BGD	74.8	BGD	64.3
LAO	93.4	LAO	99.2	LAO	97.7	KHM	77.8	MMR	72.7

Fixed telephone subscriptions (per 100 people)

Country	1980	Country	1990	Country	2000	Country	2010	Country	2016
JPN	33.9	JPN	43.8	HKG	58.9	HKG	62.1	HKG	59.1
HKG	26.0	HKG	42.8	KOR	54.6	KOR	57.6	KOR	55.2
SGP	22.2	SGP	35.0	SGP	49.7	JPN	51.0	JPN	50.2
KOR	7.1	KOR	30.9	JPN	48.6	SGP	39.3	SGP	35.5
MYS	2.9	MYS	8.8	MYS	20.0	CHN	21.6	LAO	18.7
PHL	0.9	THA	2.3	CHN	11.3	LKA	17.7	MYS	15.5
THA	0.8	PHL	1.0	THA	8.9	IDN	16.9	CHN	14.7
PAK	0.4	PAK	0.8	LKA	4.1	MYS	16.4	LKA	11.9
LKA	0.4	LKA	0.7	PHL	3.9	VNM	16.2	THA	6.8
IND	0.3	IDN	0.6	VNM	3.2	THA	10.2	VNM	5.9
IDN	0.3	CHN	0.6	IDN	3.1	PAK	3.6	IDN	4.1
CHN	0.2	IND	0.6	IND	3.1	PHL	3.6	PHL	3.7
LAO	0.2	BGD	0.2	PAK	2.2	IND	2.9	IND	1.8
BGD	0.1	MMR	0.2	LAO	0.8	KHM	2.5	PAK	1.6
VNM	0.1	LAO	0.2	MMR	0.6	LAO	1.7	KHM	1.4
MMR	0.1	VNM	0.1	BGD	0.4	MMR	1.0	MMR	1.0
KHM	0.0	KHM	0.0	KHM	0.3	BGD	0.8	BGD	0.5

Mobile cellular subscriptions (per 100 people)

Country	1980	Country	1990	Country	2000	Country	2010	Country	2016
LAO	0.0	HKG	2.3	HKG	81.7	HKG	196.3	HKG	240.8
VNM	0.0	SGP	1.7	SGP	70.2	SGP	145.5	THA	173.8
KHM	0.0	JPN	0.7	KOR	56.6	VNM	126.1	SGP	150.5
MMR	0.0	MYS	0.5	JPN	52.4	MYS	120.4	IDN	147.7
THA	0.0	KOR	0.2	MYS	22.1	THA	106.7	MYS	140.8
MYS	0.0	THA	0.1	PHL	8.3	KOR	102.5	JPN	130.6
PHL	0.0	IDN	0.0	CHN	6.6	JPN	95.9	VNM	127.5
IDN	0.0	LKA	0.0	THA	4.9	PHL	88.7	KHM	126.3
HKG	0.0	PAK	0.0	LKA	2.3	IDN	87.1	LKA	124.0
CHN	0.0	CHN	0.0	IDN	1.7	LKA	85.9	KOR	120.7
KOR	0.0	LAO	0.0	KHM	1.1	LAO	64.1	PHL	109.4
JPN	0.0	VNM	0.0	VNM	1.0	CHN	63.2	CHN	97.3
SGP	0.0	KHM	0.0	IND	0.3	IND	61.1	MMR	95.7
IND	0.0	MMR	0.0	LAO	0.2	PAK	58.2	IND	85.2
PAK	0.0	PHL	0.0	PAK	0.2	KHM	57.0	BGD	83.4
BGD	0.0	IND	0.0	BGD	0.2	BGD	44.6	PAK	70.6
LKA	0.0	BGD	0.0	MMR	0.0	MMR	1.2	LAO	58.6

Rural population growth (annual %)

Country	1980	Country	1990	Country	2000	Country	2010	Country	2016
KHM	−5.4	HKG	−62.6	MYS	−0.9	JPN	−7.9	JPN	−7.0
KOR	−2.4	KOR	−5.3	CHN	−0.8	CHN	−2.1	CHN	−2.1
HKG	−1.2	JPN	−0.2	IDN	−0.7	THA	−1.9	THA	−2.1
SGP	0.0	SGP	0.0	JPN	−0.4	MYS	−1.0	MYS	−1.2
CHN	0.3	IDN	0.4	KOR	−0.3	IDN	−0.3	IDN	−0.4
JPN	0.5	CHN	0.5	HKG	0.0	LAO	−0.2	LAO	−0.3
MYS	1.0	PHL	0.7	SGP	0.0	KOR	−0.1	KOR	−0.2
LAO	1.3	THA	1.0	VNM	0.4	MMR	−0.1	BGD	−0.1
THA	1.3	MYS	1.3	LAO	0.4	HKG	0.0	HKG	0.0
BGD	1.4	LKA	1.3	THA	0.4	SGP	0.0	SGP	0.0
IDN	1.6	MMR	1.3	LKA	0.6	BGD	0.0	MMR	0.1
LKA	1.8	VNM	1.7	MMR	0.8	VNM	0.1	VNM	0.1
IND	1.8	IND	1.7	BGD	1.5	LKA	0.6	IND	0.6
PHL	2.0	BGD	1.9	IND	1.5	IND	0.9	LKA	1.1
VNM	2.1	LAO	2.5	PAK	1.9	KHM	1.4	PAK	1.2
MMR	2.3	PAK	2.6	KHM	2.1	PAK	1.5	KHM	1.3
PAK	2.8	KHM	2.8	PHL	2.3	PHL	2.1	PHL	1.7

Life expectancy at birth, total (years)

Country	1980	Country	1990	Country	2000	Country	2010	Country	2016
JPN	76.1	JPN	78.8	JPN	81.1	HKG	83.0	HKG	84.2
HKG	74.7	HKG	77.4	HKG	80.9	JPN	82.8	JPN	84.0
SGP	72.2	SGP	75.3	SGP	78.0	SGP	81.5	SGP	82.8
LKA	68.2	KOR	71.6	KOR	75.9	KOR	80.1	KOR	82.0
MYS	68.0	MYS	70.7	VNM	73.3	CHN	75.2	VNM	76.3
VNM	67.6	VNM	70.5	MYS	72.8	VNM	75.1	CHN	76.3
CHN	66.8	THA	70.3	CHN	72.0	LKA	74.4	THA	75.3
KOR	66.0	LKA	69.5	LKA	71.0	MYS	74.2	MYS	75.3
THA	64.4	CHN	69.3	THA	70.6	THA	73.9	LKA	75.3
PHL	62.2	PHL	65.3	PHL	67.2	BGD	70.2	BGD	72.5
IDN	59.6	IDN	63.3	IDN	66.3	PHL	68.3	IDN	69.2
PAK	57.0	PAK	60.1	BGD	65.3	IDN	68.2	PHL	69.1
MMR	55.0	MMR	58.7	PAK	62.7	IND	66.6	KHM	69.0
IND	53.8	BGD	58.4	IND	62.6	KHM	66.6	IND	68.6
BGD	53.5	IND	57.9	MMR	62.1	MMR	65.2	LAO	66.7
LAO	49.1	KHM	53.6	LAO	58.9	PAK	65.1	MMR	66.6
KHM	27.5	LAO	53.6	KHM	58.4	LAO	64.4	PAK	66.5

Age dependency ratio (% of working-age population)

Country	1980	Country	1990	Country	2000	Country	2010	Country	2016
HKG	46.3	SGP	37.1	KOR	38.5	HKG	33.2	HKG	36.9
SGP	46.6	HKG	42.0	HKG	38.6	CHN	35.6	KOR	37.1
JPN	48.1	JPN	43.6	SGP	40.5	SGP	35.8	SGP	38.0
KOR	61.3	KOR	44.2	THA	43.9	KOR	36.6	CHN	38.5
LKA	67.4	CHN	52.5	CHN	46.1	THA	39.1	THA	40.1
CHN	67.8	THA	53.2	JPN	46.6	VNM	43.3	VNM	42.9
IND	75.0	LKA	60.2	LKA	49.2	LKA	48.7	MYS	44.3
MYS	75.7	IDN	67.3	IDN	54.8	MYS	49.0	IDN	48.9
THA	76.0	MYS	68.7	MMR	58.6	IDN	51.1	MMR	49.0
KHM	77.9	IND	71.7	MYS	59.4	MMR	53.6	BGD	51.5
IDN	80.7	MMR	72.2	VNM	61.5	JPN	55.9	LKA	51.5
MMR	81.4	VNM	75.8	IND	64.3	IND	56.3	IND	51.5
VNM	85.8	PHL	78.8	BGD	69.2	BGD	58.2	KHM	55.4
PHL	86.3	BGD	83.3	PHL	71.6	KHM	58.9	PHL	57.9
PAK	87.8	PAK	88.4	KHM	80.7	PHL	61.4	LAO	59.3
BGD	91.9	KHM	89.3	PAK	82.4	LAO	66.6	PAK	65.0
LAO	92.0	LAO	91.5	LAO	88.5	PAK	68.4	JPN	65.3

Survival to age 65, male (% of cohort)

Country	1980	Country	1990	Country	2000	Country	2010	Country	2016
JPN	79.6	JPN	82.6	HKG	85.5	HKG	88.2	SGP	89.6
HKG	74.9	HKG	80.7	JPN	84.8	SGP	87.8	HKG	89.3
SGP	70.7	SGP	78.2	SGP	83.4	JPN	87.2	JPN	88.3
CHN	67.8	CHN	72.1	CHN	77.2	KOR	84.2	KOR	87.0
MYS	66.2	MYS	70.4	KOR	75.8	CHN	82.0	CHN	83.5
LKA	66.0	VNM	66.7	MYS	73.8	MYS	75.1	MYS	76.5
VNM	62.0	THA	66.2	VNM	69.2	LKA	71.9	VNM	73.1
IDN	57.5	KOR	65.7	BGD	66.3	VNM	71.1	LKA	73.1
THA	57.4	LKA	63.6	LKA	65.9	THA	70.6	BGD	73.0
PAK	55.6	IDN	61.5	THA	65.6	BGD	70.5	THA	72.6
PHL	54.9	PAK	59.4	IDN	64.0	PAK	66.0	PAK	67.6
KOR	54.9	BGD	59.2	PAK	62.6	IDN	65.5	KHM	67.3
BGD	52.6	PHL	57.6	PHL	59.6	IND	64.4	IDN	67.1
IND	47.1	IND	52.3	IND	58.8	KHM	63.7	IND	66.8
MMR	45.1	MMR	51.0	MMR	56.6	MMR	61.4	LAO	65.0
LAO	38.2	LAO	44.7	LAO	52.8	LAO	61.3	MMR	63.3
KHM	19.9	KHM	42.1	KHM	52.5	PHL	60.5	PHL	61.6

Physicians (per 1,000 people)

Country	1980	Country	1990	Country	2000	Country	2010	Country	2016
JPN	1.3	JPN	1.7	JPN	2.0	JPN	2.2	CHN	3.6
CHN	1.2	SGP	1.3	SGP	1.4	KOR	2.0	JPN	2.4
SGP	0.9	CHN	1.1	HKG	1.3	SGP	1.7	KOR	2.3
HKG	0.8	HKG	1.1	KOR	1.3	HKG	1.6	SGP	2.3
KOR	0.5	KOR	0.8	CHN	1.3	CHN	1.5	HKG	2.2
IND	0.4	PAK	0.5	MYS	0.7	MYS	1.2	MYS	1.5
PAK	0.3	IND	0.4	PAK	0.7	PHL	1.1	PHL	1.1
MYS	0.3	VNM	0.4	PHL	0.6	PAK	0.9	PAK	1.0
VNM	0.2	MYS	0.4	IND	0.5	LKA	0.7	LKA	0.9
MMR	0.2	LAO	0.2	VNM	0.5	VNM	0.7	VNM	0.8
THA	0.1	THA	0.2	LKA	0.4	IND	0.7	IND	0.8
LKA	0.1	BGD	0.2	THA	0.4	MMR	0.5	MMR	0.6
PHL	0.1	IDN	0.1	MMR	0.3	THA	0.4	LAO	0.5
BGD	0.1	LKA	0.1	LAO	0.3	BGD	0.4	BGD	0.5
IDN	0.1	PHL	0.1	BGD	0.2	LAO	0.3	THA	0.5
KHM	0.1	KHM	0.1	KHM	0.2	KHM	0.2	IDN	0.2
LAO	0.1	MMR	0.1	IDN	0.2	IDN	0.1	KHM	0.1

Machinery and transport equipment (% of value added in manufacturing)

Country	1980	Country	1990	Country	2000	Country	2010	Country	2016
JPN	21.2	SGP	30.4	SGP	56.9	SGP	54.6	LAO	..
SGP	20.5	KOR	30.2	KOR	41.3	KOR	50.1	VNM	..
CHN	18.5	JPN	24.9	MYS	37.8	JPN	37.5	KHM	..
IND	16.9	IND	17.5	JPN	33.9	HKG	31.5	MMR	..
KOR	9.3	CHN	15.5	THA	25.9	PHL	30.5	THA	..
IDN	8.0	HKG	11.7	PHL	24.9	MYS	27.8	MYS	..
MYS	7.5	THA	10.0	IDN	20.2	IDN	22.4	PHL	..
PHL	6.8	MYS	9.3	IND	15.6	IND	19.1	IDN	..
PAK	5.8	IDN	8.8	CHN	14.1	VNM	14.7	HKG	..
HKG	5.0	PAK	5.2	VNM	11.8	LKA	2.3	CHN	..
THA	3.7	PHL	3.9	HKG	11.7	LAO	..	KOR	..
LKA	2.5	BGD	3.6	LAO	8.0	KHM	..	JPN	..
BGD	1.8	LKA	3.3	PAK	4.6	MMR	..	SGP	..
LAO	0.0	LAO	0.0	LKA	4.0	THA	..	IND	..
VNM	0.0	VNM	0.0	BGD	3.3	CHN	..	PAK	..
KHM	0.0	KHM	0.0	KHM	0.1	PAK	..	BGD	..
MMR	0.0	MMR	0.0	MMR	..	BGD	..	LKA	..

Gross fixed capital formation, private sector (% of GDP)

Country	1980	Country	1990	Country	2000	Country	2010	Country	2016
SGP	34.5	THA	34.2	SGP	27.0	CHN	35.0	CHN	32.9
HKG	27.4	KOR	28.7	LKA	24.8	VNM	26.6	MMR	26.3
LKA	24.3	SGP	26.7	CHN	23.4	IND	25.3	BGD	23.0
KOR	24.0	JPN	24.4	KOR	22.6	BGD	21.6	IDN	22.6
JPN	24.0	HKG	22.8	HKG	21.6	KOR	21.5	LKA	21.6
PHL	21.8	MYS	21.9	VNM	21.6	SGP	21.1	PHL	21.3
MYS	20.5	LKA	18.0	JPN	19.8	IDN	21.0	LAO	21.2
CHN	19.3	PHL	17.7	IND	17.6	HKG	18.1	KOR	20.7
THA	18.9	IDN	16.7	BGD	17.3	THA	17.9	SGP	19.9
BGD	12.1	IND	15.2	PHL	15.9	LAO	17.7	IND	19.7
IND	9.9	CHN	14.6	THA	13.5	LKA	17.6	JPN	18.1
IDN	9.6	LAO	10.5	MYS	13.4	PHL	17.2	THA	17.8
MMR	8.0	BGD	9.5	KHM	11.9	JPN	16.2	VNM	17.7
VNM	7.2	PAK	8.9	PAK	10.3	MMR	14.9	MYS	17.2
PAK	6.4	MMR	8.0	IDN	8.6	MYS	12.3	HKG	16.6
KHM	6.0	VNM	7.2	MMR	8.0	PAK	10.5	KHM	14.1
LAO	3.2	KHM	6.0	LAO	6.3	KHM	9.7	PAK	10.2

School enrollment, secondary (% gross)

Country	1980	Country	1990	Country	2000	Country	2010	Country	2016
VNM	43.4	JPN	94.7	JPN	99.4	JPN	100.4	THA	120.6
THA	27.8	KOR	92.9	KOR	96.0	LKA	96.9	VNM	117.6
SGP	61.1	HKG	73.8	HKG	79.4	KOR	96.3	HKG	102.7
PHL	65.5	SGP	73.8	SGP	79.4	CHN	88.0	SGP	102.7
PAK	17.0	PHL	72.0	LKA	76.5	HKG	87.3	JPN	102.1
MYS	54.7	LKA	72.0	PHL	74.5	SGP	87.3	KOR	100.2
MMR	21.4	MYS	63.4	MYS	69.8	PHL	84.1	LKA	97.7
LKA	53.6	IDN	46.6	THA	62.8	THA	82.4	CHN	95.0
LAO	18.4	CHN	37.4	CHN	59.7	MYS	80.2	PHL	88.3
KOR	75.6	IND	37.3	VNM	57.8	VNM	79.4	IDN	86.0
KHM	18.4	VNM	34.8	IDN	55.1	IDN	74.5	MYS	85.2
JPN	91.6	THA	28.5	BGD	48.0	IND	63.3	IND	75.2
IND	29.0	KHM	27.9	IND	45.1	BGD	50.0	BGD	69.0
IDN	28.3	LAO	23.2	MMR	37.4	MMR	49.5	LAO	66.5
HKG	61.1	PAK	22.0	LAO	34.1	LAO	46.8	MMR	60.5
CHN	43.0	BGD	20.4	PAK	22.8	KHM	45.2	PAK	46.1
BGD	18.5	MMR	20.0	KHM	17.3	PAK	35.8	KHM	45.2

Mortality rate, infant (per 1,000 live births)

Country	1980	Country	1990	Country	2000	Country	2010	Country	2016
JPN	7.4	JPN	4.6	HKG	3.0	HKG	2.2	JPN	2.0
HKG	11.9	HKG	6.2	SGP	3.0	SGP	2.2	HKG	2.2
SGP	11.9	SGP	6.2	JPN	3.3	JPN	2.4	SGP	2.2
MYS	25.7	KOR	13.5	KOR	6.4	KOR	3.5	KOR	2.9
KOR	29.7	MYS	14.3	MYS	8.7	MYS	6.8	MYS	7.1
LKA	39.7	LKA	17.9	LKA	14.1	LKA	9.7	LKA	8.0
VNM	46.4	THA	30.9	THA	19.6	THA	12.8	CHN	8.5
THA	47.3	VNM	36.7	VNM	23.6	CHN	13.5	THA	10.5
CHN	48.2	PHL	40.8	PHL	30.0	VNM	18.6	VNM	17.3
PHL	53.4	CHN	42.2	CHN	30.1	PHL	24.9	PHL	21.5
IDN	85.0	IDN	62.0	IDN	41.1	IDN	27.5	IDN	22.2
MMR	97.8	MMR	81.8	BGD	64.0	KHM	37.8	KHM	26.3
IND	114.3	KHM	84.8	MMR	65.6	BGD	39.1	BGD	28.2
KHM	116.2	IND	88.4	IND	66.6	IND	45.5	IND	34.6
PAK	124.0	BGD	99.7	KHM	79.6	MMR	49.3	MMR	40.1
BGD	133.6	PAK	106.2	LAO	82.5	LAO	58.5	LAO	48.9
LAO	135.5	LAO	110.7	PAK	88.1	PAK	73.6	PAK	64.2

Principal component

Country	1980	Country	1990	Country	2000	Country	2010	Country	2016
JPN	5.3	HKG	5.8	HKG	5.2	HKG	4.8	HKG	4.7
HKG	4.3	SGP	4.8	SGP	4.9	SGP	4.0	SGP	3.8
SGP	4.3	JPN	4.8	JPN	4.0	KOR	3.5	KOR	3.1
KOR	2.0	KOR	2.6	KOR	3.8	JPN	3.3	JPN	2.9
CHN	1.2	MYS	0.9	CHN	1.4	CHN	2.4	CHN	2.4
MYS	0.7	THA	0.7	MYS	1.1	THA	1.0	THA	1.5
LKA	0.5	CHN	0.6	THA	0.3	MYS	0.8	MYS	0.6
THA	−0.2	LKA	0.0	LKA	0.2	VNM	0.3	VNM	0.2
PHL	−0.3	PHL	−0.8	VNM	−0.3	LKA	0.1	LKA	−0.2
VNM	−0.7	IDN	−1.0	IDN	−1.0	IDN	−0.9	IDN	−0.7
IDN	−1.3	VNM	−1.5	PHL	−1.2	PHL	−1.4	PHL	−1.7
IND	−1.7	IND	−1.8	IND	−1.9	IND	−1.8	IND	−1.8
PAK	−2.4	PAK	−2.6	BGD	−2.4	BGD	−2.3	BGD	−1.9
MMR	−2.4	BGD	−2.8	MMR	−2.6	MMR	−3.2	MMR	−2.7
BGD	−2.5	MMR	−2.8	PAK	−3.2	KHM	−3.3	LAO	−3.1
KHM	−3.1	KHM	−3.2	LAO	−4.1	LAO	−3.6	KHM	−3.1
LAO	−3.6	LAO	−3.7	KHM	−4.2	PAK	−3.8	PAK	-4.1

References

Anselin, L. (1988), *Spatial Econometrics: Methods and Models,* Dordrecht: Kluwer.

Brunner, H., and M. Calí (2006), "The Dynamics of Manufacturing Competitiveness in South Asia: An Analysis through Export Data," *Journal of Asian Economics,* 17(4), pp.557-582.

Cai, F. (2012), "The Coming Demographic Impact on China's Growth: The Age Factor in the Middle-Income Trap," *Asian Economic Papers,* 11(1), pp.95-111.

Erber, G., H. Hagemann, and S. Seiter (1997), "Global Competitiveness: Industrial Policy in the Performance of Asia and Europe," *Journal of Contemporary Asia,* 3, pp.338-355.

Hall, R., and C. Jones (1999), "Why Do Some Countries Produce So Much More Output per Worker Than Others?" *Quarterly Journal of Economics,* 114(1), pp.83-116.

Huang, X. (2007), "Institutional Competitiveness and Institutional Aging: The Dynamism of East Asian Growth," *Journal of the Asia Pacific Economy,* 13(1), pp.3-25.

International Institute for Management Development (IMD) (2017), *World Competitiveness Yearbook 2017.*

Japan Center for Economic Research (JCER) (2011), *Potential Competitiveness Ranking 2010.*

Oral, M., and H. Chabchoub (1996), "On the Methodology of the World Competitiveness Report," *European Journal of Operational Research,* 90(3), pp.514-535.

Petrarca, F., and S. Terzi (2018), "The Global Competitiveness Index: An Alternative Measure with Endogenously Derived Weights," *Quality & Quantity* (https://doi.org/10.1007/s11135-017-0655-8).

Williamson, P., S. Hoenderop, and J. Hoenderop (2018), "An Alternative Benchmark for the Validity of China's GDP Growth Statistics," *Journal of Chinese Economic and Business Studies,* 16(2), pp.171-191.

World Economic Forum (WEF) (2016), *The Global Competitiveness Report 2017-2018.*

Yamasawa, N. (2013), "The Middle-Income Trap Verified by Data: The Exit Key is Developing Institutions," *The ASEAN Economy and the Middle-Income Trap, Japan Center for Economic Research,* pp.17-30.

Zhang, W., and T. Zhang (2005), "Competitiveness of China's Manufacturing Industry and its Impacts on the Neighbouring Countries," *Journal of Chinese Economic and Business Studies,* 3(3), pp.205-229.